CONTEMPORARY
CLASS PIANO
SECOND EDITION

CONTEMPORARY CLASS PIANO

SECOND EDITION

ELYSE MACH

Northeastern Illinois University

HBJ HARCOURT BRACE JOVANOVICH, INC.

New York/San Diego/Chicago/San Francisco/Atlanta/London/Sydney/Toronto

Photo credits

cover, Molly Frederick
page 2, Mike Tappin, Northeastern Illinois University Learning Services

ISBN: 0-15-513480-9

Library of Congress Catalog Card Number: 81-83814

Printed in the United States of America

To my sons
Sean, Aaron, and Andrew

PREFACE

Contemporary Class Piano, now in its second edition, is an introduction to the keyboard designed for college students who are enrolled in a class piano course, whether or not they are music majors and whether or not they have any prior keyboard experience. It is suitable for prospective elementary teachers, for nonpiano majors who must gain keyboard proficiency, and for any student who wishes to learn how to play the piano for the sheer fun of it. The book has been distilled from seventeen years of experience in developing and teaching the class piano program at Northestern Illinois University.

The book's creative and multidimensional approach made its first edition a great success in class piano courses throughout the country. Besides offering an abundant solo and ensemble repertoire—including classical pieces from the Baroque to the contemporary period, and folk, jazz, pop, and blues tunes—the book teaches students to sight read, to transpose, to improvise in various styles, to harmonize folk and popular songs, and to compose simple accompanied melodies. In addition, students learn the fundamentals of theory and musical form. Throughout, all materials are presented with a logical progression in difficulty.

The text is divided into six units. Unit 1 introduces keyboard basics and the five-finger position. The emphasis is on learning to play by touch, without looking down at the keys. Note reading is taught by interval study, and a multikey approach to reading is stressed. A section at the end of this and subsequent units is devoted to sightreading studies, improvisation, creative activities, and ensemble pieces, all reinforcing techniques and skills introduced in the unit.

Unit 2 contains many simple pieces based on the five-finger position. Throughout this unit and the next, a register guide appears at the beginning of every piece to help students quickly locate the correct starting position in both hands.

Unit 3 extends the five-finger position and offers students an unusually large variety of accompaniment patterns for improvisation and creative writing.

Unit 4 contains minor and modal materials, but it is largely devoted to twentieth-century pieces, introducing students to pandiatonicism, clusters, innovative notations, and polytonal, atonal, and twelve-tone pieces and techniques.

Unit 5 provides students with practice in harmonizing folk and popular melodies with various accompaniment patterns. The interpretation of letter-name chord symbols is an important feature of this unit.

Unit 6 is an anthology of twenty-five pieces by representative composers of the standard repertoire, pieces that vary widely in difficulty, length, and style. The compositions are presented in their original form, with no changes except for fingerings and slight editing where necessary to aid the player. For students who advance quickly, these pieces will provide a special challenge; they also provide ample material for a second year of piano study.

The second edition retains all the strengths of the first, and it has been enriched in several respects. More "now-sound" pieces, more classical and twentieth-century compositions—some with innovative notations—a more representative selection of minor and modal pieces, and several favorite popular melodies for harmonizing have been added to the solo repertoire. The ensemble repertoire has been expanded to include four- and eight-hand arrangements of master twentieth-century repertoire as well as popular tunes from Broadway musicals. New theory concepts and study techniques—secondary chords, primary and secondary chord progressions, interval classifications, cluster scales, open-fifth and triad studies—are introduced. Lists of important terms for review have been added to Units 1-4, and an index is now included.

I am grateful to the following people for their efforts and help in the preparation of the second edition: Albert Richards of Harcourt Brace Jovanovich, for his steadfast professional support and his gracious assistance throughout this entire project; Natalie Bowen, my editor at Harcourt Brace Jovanovich, whom I could not do without for her fine professional expertise, her enthusiasm and encouragement, and her incredible ability to always make the right comment or suggestion; Laurene Heimann, University of Texas at Austin; Ronald Regal, Ithaca College; Nancy J. Stephenson, University of Houston, and Madelene Zachary, University of Arkansas, for reviewing the manuscript and providing valuable critical judgment; my husband, John, for his many useful ideas on visual materials; and William James, Glenn Jenne, and Ella Marks, for their generous help in the acquisition of pertinent music materials. Finally, to my colleagues and students I offer special thanks for providing me with new musical insights for this second edition.

ELYSE MACH

CONTENTS

CONTEMPORARY CLASS PIANO
SECOND EDITION

1

KEYBOARD BASICS

Your **body** should be far enough back from the keyboard so that it bends slightly forward at the waist, as in the left-hand photograph on page 2. Don't try to maintain an absolutely straight sitting position.

Your **arms** should hang loosely and rather quietly at your sides. Try not to point your elbows away from the sides of your body.

Your **wrists** should be level with the keys so that your hand can fall from the wrist. Try not to allow your wrists to slump below the keyboard level.

Your **hands** should be slightly cupped as if you were holding a bubble in each hand. They should remain as motionless as possible. Don't move your hands up and down to strike each key as if you were "pumping" the notes. Think of your hands as floating above the keys rather than sticking to them.

Your **fingers** should be curved so that each key is struck with the ball or fleshy part of the finger. *Keep your fingers as close to the keys as possible.* Don't allow them to point upward at any time. Strike the keys instead of pressing them down.

As soon as possible, your **eyes** should look away from the keys as you play. Learn to develop a "feel" for the keys—that is, learn to play by touch.

These two photographs illustrate the correct keyboard position for body, arms, wrists, hands, and fingers.

THE KEYBOARD

The standard piano keyboard has 88 keys, but only the first seven letters of the alphabet—A, B, C, D, E, F, G—are used to name the white keys.

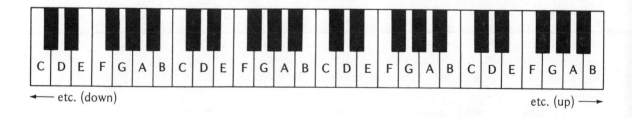

← etc. (down)   etc. (up) →

Practice playing the musical alphabet up and down the keyboard until you are familiar with the names and location of the white keys. Do this first with the right hand, then with the left, using whatever finger is most comfortable for you. As you move to the right, you will be playing higher **tones** or **pitches**. As you move to the left, you will be playing lower pitches.

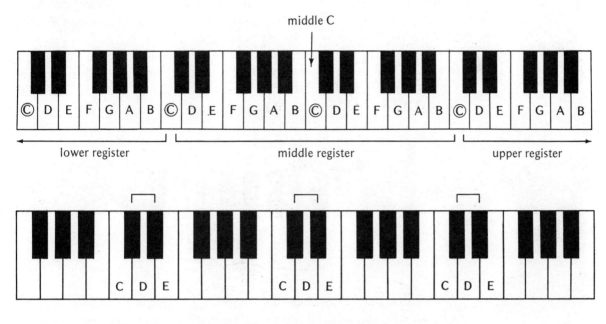

Next play the musical alphabet in different **registers**—segments of the total range of the keyboard—lower register, middle register, and upper register, as in the following diagram. (Middle C is the C nearest the center of the keyboard.)

Pick out all the groups of two black keys on the keyboard both upward and downward using the right hand first and then the left hand.

Notice that three white keys—C, D, E—are located around the groups of two black keys in the following order:

C is to the left of the two black keys.
D is between the two black keys.
E is to the right of the two black keys.

Using the groups of two black keys as reference points, pick out all the C's and E's, then all the D's.

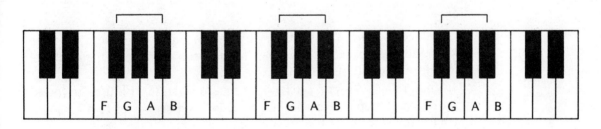

Next pick out all the groups of three black keys using the right hand first and then the left hand.

Four white keys—F, G, A, B—are located around the groups of three black keys in the following order:

F is to the left of the three black keys.
G is between the first and second keys in the group of three black keys.
A is between the second and third keys in the group of three black keys.
B is to the right of the three black keys.

Using the groups of three black keys as reference points, pick out all the F's and B's. Practice the rest of the tones in the same manner.

After you have learned the keys by sight, start to locate them by *touch*—that is, learn to find any key without looking down. First, without looking down, pick out all the groups of two black keys. Next pick out all the groups of three black keys. Using these black-key groupings as reference points, start picking out individual tones.

A **sharp** (♯) raises a pitch one half step. A **half step** is the distance from one key to the nearest key, either up or down, either white or black. For example, C to C♯, E to E♯, A♯ to A, and B♯ to B are all half steps. Note that E♯ and B♯ are white-key sharps.

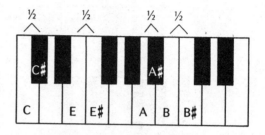

Practice playing half steps from middle C upward to the next C and then back down again. Recite the letter names as you play them.

A **flat** (♭) lowers a pitch one half step. For example, B to B♭, F to F♭, and C to C♭ are all half steps. Note that F♭ and C♭ are white-key flats.

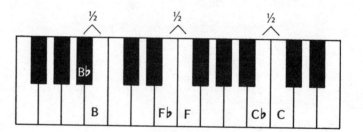

Practice playing half steps beginning on middle C downward to the next C and then back up again. Recite the letter names and their half-step relationships as you play them.

A **natural** (♮) brings a pitch to its unaltered state. It is used to lower a pitch one half step if the note has already been raised, or to raise a pitch one half step if the note has already been lowered.

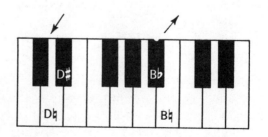

The black keys use the same letter names as the white, but with the addition of either a sharp or a flat. The name of a black key is taken from the white key on either side of it. Each black key, then, has two names. For example, the black key between F and G is called either F♯ or G♭. F♯ and G♭ are called **enharmonic tones** since they are the same pitch but are referred to by different names.

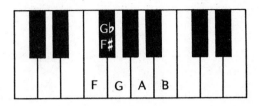

What are the two names of the black key between G and A? between A and B?

The seven white-key pitches and the five black-key pitches make up the total of twelve tones with which our music is written.

Play the following tones, and recite their names. Then name the pairs of tones that are enharmonic.

G,   G♯,   G♭
C,   C♯,   C♭
F,   F♯,   F♭
A,   A♯,   A♭
D,   D♯,   D♭
E,   E♯,   E♭
B,   B♯,   B♭

FINGER NUMBERS

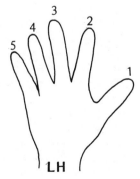

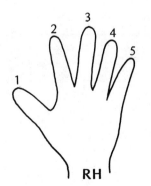

Because good fingering is a prerequisite to facility at the keyboard, you should learn the finger numbers right away. Practice various finger-number combinations by tapping on the wood panel over the piano keys, first with each hand separately, then with both hands. Remember that the two thumbs are 1, the two index fingers are 2, the two middle fingers are 3, and so on.

THE FIVE-FINGER PATTERN

The **five-finger pattern** is a particular combination of half steps and whole steps.

A **whole step** is a combination of two half steps. For example, E♭ to F is a whole step, A to B is a whole step, and C♯ to D♯ is a whole step.

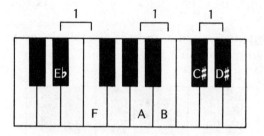

Practice playing and saying whole steps up and down the keyboard.

The five-finger pattern can be constructed on any of the twelve tones. The first tone of the five-finger pattern is referred to as the **tonic**. If we build the pattern on G♭, G♭ is the tonic. This is the way the five-finger pattern is constructed:

> first tone: tonic
> second tone: whole step up
> third tone: whole step up
> fourth tone: half step up
> fifth tone: whole step up

The five-finger pattern is the first five tones of a major scale (to be discussed in Unit 3). Here is the five-finger pattern in C:

Five-finger pattern in C

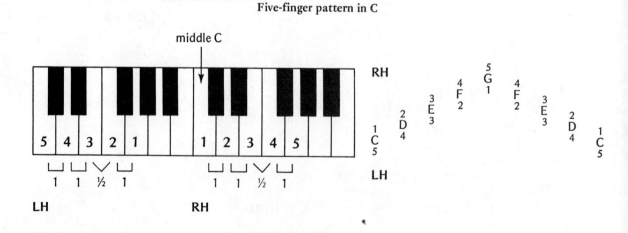

Practice the five-finger patterns in C, and also in G, G♭, and F, diagrams for which are given below. Select several other tones as your starting tone or tonic as well, using the whole step-half step construction guide to help you as you start learning them.

Play the patterns first with each hand separately ascending and descending. Next play the patterns with both hands moving in the same direction (**parallel motion**). Then play the same patterns with your hands moving in opposite directions, with the thumbs beginning together (**contrary motion**). Play the patterns **legato**—that is, connect the tones so that they sound as smooth as possible.

Five-finger pattern in G

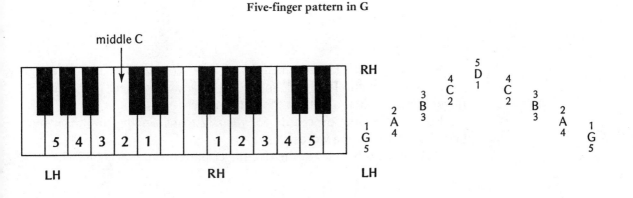

Five-finger pattern in G♭

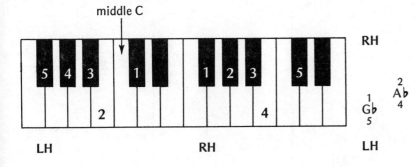

Five-finger pattern in F

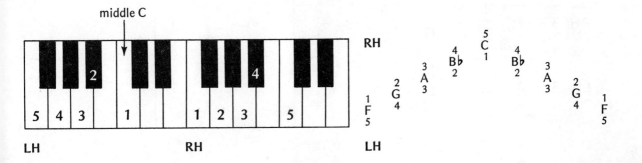

Ode to Joy and Lightly Row can be played using the tones of the five-finger pattern.

First find the five-finger pattern of C:

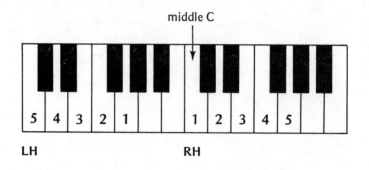

Next sing and play the melody of Ode to Joy—first with the right hand, then with the left, and finally with hands together. Try singing the finger numbers first, and then the letter names.

Follow the same procedure for Lightly Row, singing the finger numbers first and then the words.

Now play both tunes in the five-finger patterns of G, G♭, and F.

ODE TO JOY*

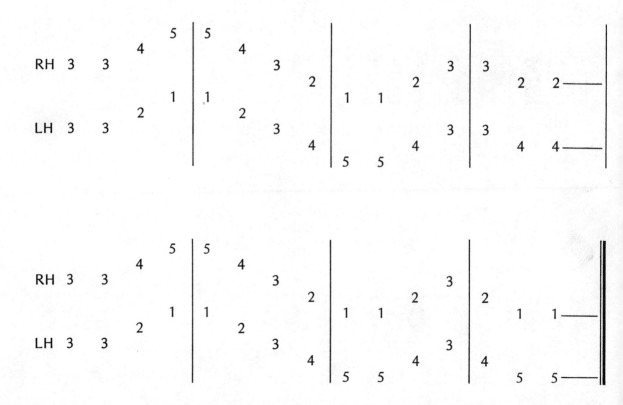

*Ode to Joy appears in notated form on page 22.

LIGHTLY ROW

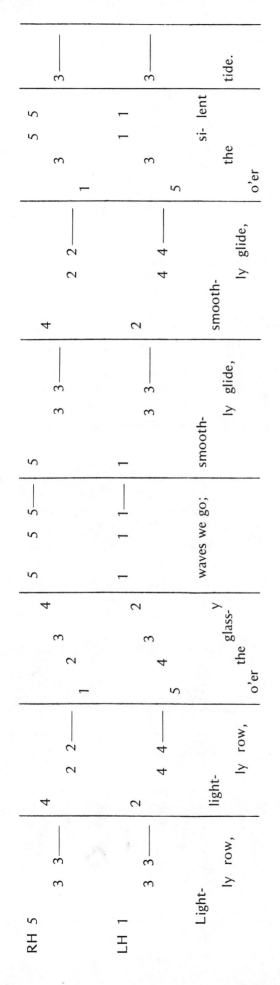

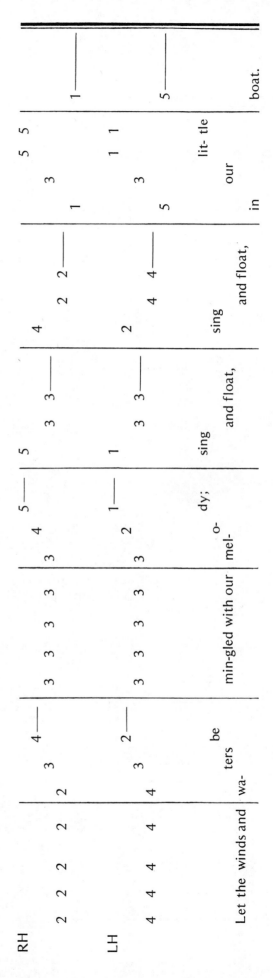

READING NOTES

The Staff and Clefs

A **staff** consists of five lines and four spaces, to which a **clef** is added to indicate the pitches of the notes.

The **treble clef** or **G clef** sign fixes the position of the G above middle C on the second line upward, which one of the curves on the clef encircles:

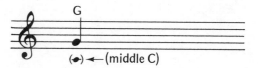

The **bass clef** or **F clef** sign fixes the position of the F below middle C on the fourth line upward, which is enclosed by two dots:

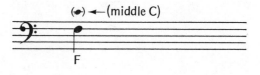

The right hand usually plays the notes in the treble clef, to the right of middle C, and the left hand usually plays the notes in the bass clef, to the left of middle C.

The **grand staff**, also called the **great staff**, is made up of two staffs, one with a treble clef, the other with a bass clef. The short lines above and below the staff are called **leger lines**. Their purpose is to extend the range of the staffs when necessary:

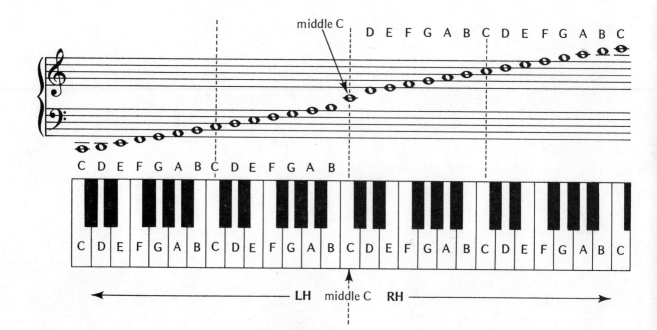

Note that although both the treble and bass clefs use the same letters and arrangement of letters, *the location of letters differs from one clef to another.* For example, the second space from the bottom in the treble clef is A, but in the bass clef the second space from the bottom is C, not A.

Beginning with C, second space in the bass clef, play and name the bass clef notes up to middle C and then back down again. Next, beginning on middle C, play and name the notes upward in the treble clef to the next C and then back down again. Memorize these note names and their location on the grand staff as quickly as possible. Once you have learned these notes, learn the rest of the notes on the staff.

Name and play the following treble-clef notes:

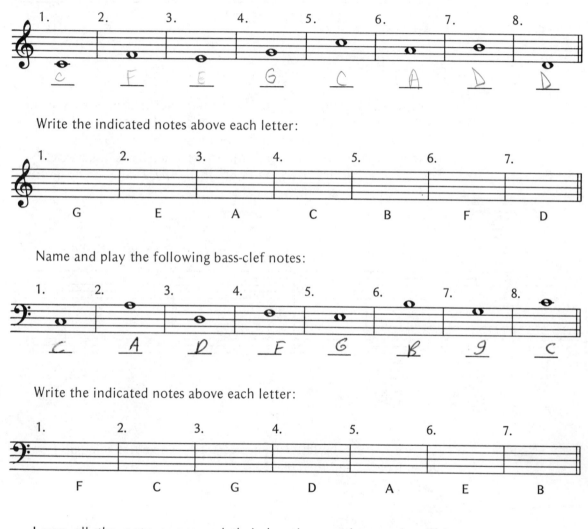

Write the indicated notes above each letter:

Name and play the following bass-clef notes:

Write the indicated notes above each letter:

Learn all the note names and their location on the grand staff by memorizing the line notes and space notes in the treble and bass clefs.

Treble clef

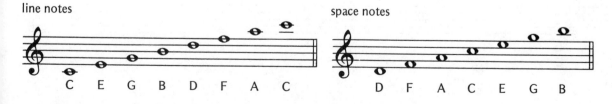

Practice naming the line notes in the treble clef first upward and then downward. Next name and play the line notes in the same manner. Then begin picking out individual line notes of your choice.

Follow the same procedure in learning the space notes in treble clef.

Bass clef

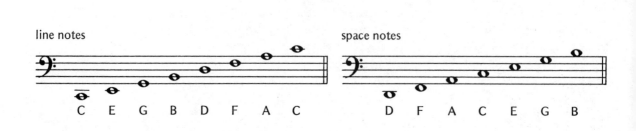

line notes

C E G B D F A C

space notes

D F A C E G B

Practice naming the line notes in the bass clef first upward and then downward. Next name and play the line notes in the bass clef in the same manner. Then begin picking out individual line notes of your choice.

Follow the same procedure in learning the space notes in bass clef.

Practice writing the letter names of all the *space* notes going up from D and down from B, and then play them:

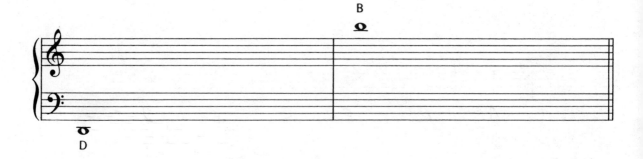

B

D

Practice writing the letter names of all the *line* notes going up from C and down from C, and then play them:

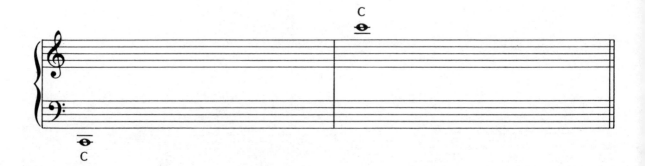

C

C

Play *Love Somebody,* using the five-finger pattern in G:

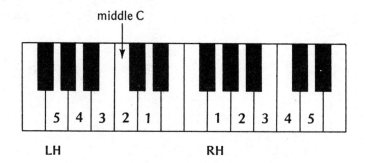

LOVE SOMEBODY

American

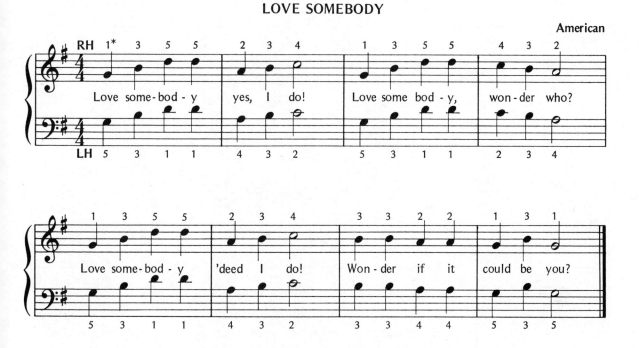

Since *Love Somebody* uses the five-finger pattern constructed on G, we can say that it is written in the **key** of G. G is our tonic or **key note.**

The **key signature** appears after the clef signs and indicates the notes which should be played as sharps or flats throughout a piece—that is, the key signature helps to indicate the key of a piece.

Now play this piece in the key of F. Playing a piece in a different key (a different five-finger pattern) is called **transposition.** You are transposing this piece into the key of F. Play it in the key of G♭, too, and other keys of your choice.

*These small numbers are finger numbers. They will not always be provided in full as they are here, because soon you will be so familiar with the five-finger patterns that you will not need complete fingerings.

Intervals

Good reading habits in music are developed by learning to read notes in relationship to each other—that is, recognizing the distance between notes. This is called reading by interval.

An **interval** is the distance between two notes. For example: C to F is a fourth because counting upward by letter name, C is 1 and F is 4.

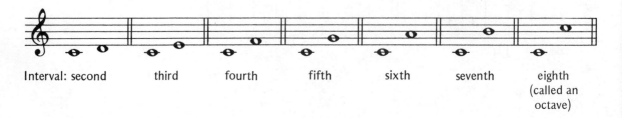

Interval: second   third   fourth   fifth   sixth   seventh   eighth
(called an octave)

Melodic intervals are written and played one note following the other:

Harmonic intervals are written and played together:

Practice building various melodic and harmonic intervals starting on C, first with the right hand, then with the left hand, and finally with both hands.

Read the following intervals and then try playing them without looking down at the keyboard as you move from one note to the next—that is, concentrate on developing a "feel" for the distance between the various intervals.

Name and play these intervals with the right hand:

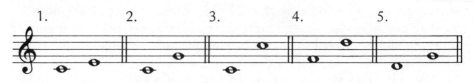

Name and play these intervals with the left hand:

Now play the intervals with both hands, placing the hands one octave apart from each other.

Construct the given interval *up* from the given note; next, write the letter names on the blanks below, then play the intervals with the right hand.

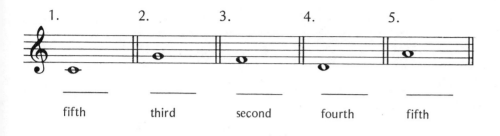

| fifth | third | second | fourth | fifth |

Name and play the intervals given:

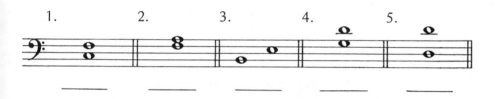

Construct the given interval *down* from the given note; next, write the letter names on the blanks below, and then play these intervals with the left hand.

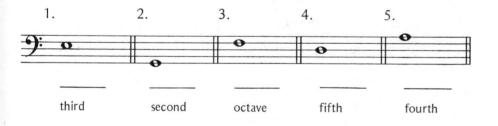

| third | second | octave | fifth | fourth |

Name and play the intervals given:

Below are some of the melody notes of well-known pieces. Pick out these notes at the keyboard. As you do so, study the interval patterns. Play with the right hand:

Ode to Joy (Beethoven)

Jingle Bells

Play with the left hand:

The Star-Spangled Banner

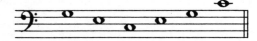

Red River Valley

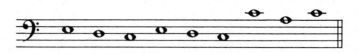

Swanee River

KEEPING TIME

Meter and Tempo

Music usually has a regular pulse. **Meter** is the grouping of strong and weak **pulses** (or **beats**) into a regularly recurring pattern. For example:

Duple meter has groupings of two—a strong beat
followed by a weak one:

1 2 **1** 2

Triple meter has groupings of three—a strong beat
followed by two weak ones:

1 2 3 **1** 2 3

Quadruple meter has groupings of four—a strong beat
followed by three weak ones (sometimes the third
beat is slightly accented):

1 2 *3* 4 **1** 2 *3* 4

The staff is marked off by vertical bar lines into **measures** (or **bars**) of
these regular beats. A **double bar line** indicates the end of a piece. At the
beginning of a piece you will find a **meter signature**—two numbers that
look something like a fraction. The top number indicates the number of
beats in a measure, and the bottom number indicates the kind of note that
receives one beat. The quarter note is the most common unit of beat, but
other notes are also used.

Here are some examples of meter signatures:

$\frac{4}{4}$ —four beats to the measure
the quarter note (♩) receives one beat

$\frac{3}{4}$ —three beats to the measure
the quarter note receives one beat

$\frac{2}{4}$ —two beats to the measure
the quarter note receives one beat

$\frac{6}{8}$ —six beats to the measure
the eighth note (♪) receives one beat

Play and count the example below:

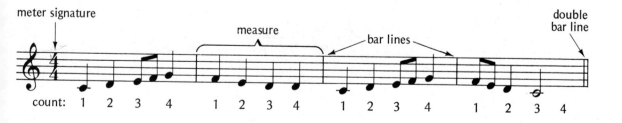

Tempo is the rate of movement or speed. Note values are always relative, depending on the tempo. For example, a quarter note will be held
longer in a slow tempo than it would in a fast tempo.

Note Values and Rests

Rhythm is a particular arrangement of note values and rests. A **rest** represents a silence of the same length as the value of its corresponding note. Here are the most commonly used notes and rests:

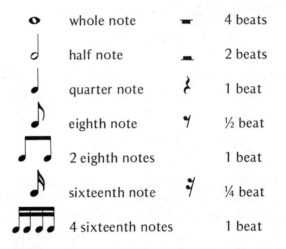

Play and count the following rhythmic patterns. Until you are familiar with the patterns, subdivide the quarter-note beat as shown by the plus signs, saying aloud "one and two and three and," and so forth. Plus signs in parentheses are optional subdivisions.

5.

count: 1   2   3   4 (+) 1 + 2 + 3 + 4 +   1 (+)

6.

count: 1 (+) 2 + 3 (+) 4

7.

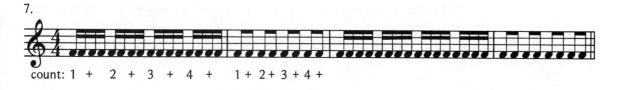

count: 1 + 2 + 3 + 4 +   1 + 2 + 3 + 4 +

A **dot** placed after a note increases its value by one half:

Examples: 𝅗𝅥. = 3 beats (a 𝅗𝅥 plus a ♩)

♩. = 1½ beats (a ♩ plus an ♪)

Play and count the following examples:

count: 1   2   3   1   2   3   1   2   3   1   2 + 3

count: 1   2   3   1   2 + 3   1   2 + 3   1   2   3

A curved line connecting two adjacent notes of the same pitch is called a **tie**. The second note is not sounded; instead, it is sustained (held) for the duration of its value. The tied F below is held for three beats in all:

Example:

1   2   3

Study the rhythmic and melodic patterns in *Little Song.* Play it in the key of G♭, the five-finger pattern of which is given below:

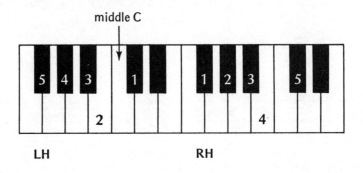

Try transposing this piece to the key of G, starting on B with the third finger of each hand.

LITTLE SONG

Antonio Diabelli (1781-1858)

■ **C** is the same as $\frac{4}{4}$.

■ **Piano** (***p***) is a dynamic marking that means to play softly.

The piece *Sweet Rock* uses eighth-note rhythmic patterns. Remember that two eighth notes are equal to one quarter note and should be played *evenly* in one beat. When two eighth notes are paired together, a **beam** is used.

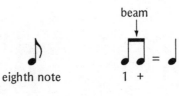

First count the eighth notes like this:

Once you are able to feel the beat divided into two equal parts, count, as follows:

Practice clapping and counting the rhythm that appears in *Sweet Rock*. After you have studied the rhythmic and melodic patterns, play it in the key in which it is written. What five-finger pattern is used?

Try playing this piece in various other keys, always starting with the tonic tone of each five-finger pattern.

SWEET ROCK

E.M.

■ **Forte** (*f*) is a dynamic marking that means to play loud.

Study the rhythmic pattern ♩. ♪♩ that appears in *Ode to Joy*. Isolate this pattern and count as you clap:

♩.   ♪♩
1   2 + 3 4

Next stamp your foot on the second beat as you clap the rhythmic pattern. Try to feel the pulse of the beat and the dotted rhythm.

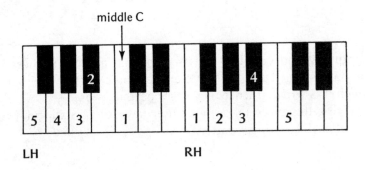

After you have studied the rhythmic and melodic patterns for the *Ode to Joy*, play it in the key of F, the five-finger pattern of which is given below:

Play the piece in various other keys as well, always starting with the third finger of each hand.

ODE TO JOY (from the Ninth Symphony)

Ludwig van Beethoven (1770–1827) (arr. E. M.)

- **Mezzo forte** (*mf*) is a dynamic marking that means to play moderately loud.

- **Mezzo piano** (*mp*) is a dynamic marking that means to play moderately soft.

IMPROVISATION

Pentatonic Improvisation

Using the **pentatonic scale** (a five-tone scale built on the black keys only) is an excellent way to begin improvising because it is impossible to play a wrong note! Since all sounds produced on the black keys blend, it is both fun and easy to improvise many different tunes and styles.

Using the black keys only, pick out some of the melodies listed below. The starting note for each is given in parentheses.

> *Merrily We Roll Along* (B♭)
> *Peter, Peter, Pumpkin-Eater* (B♭)
> *Auld Lang Syne* (D♭)
> *Old MacDonald Had a Farm* (G♭)
> *Arkansas Traveler* (G♭)
> *Nobody Knows the Trouble I've Seen* (B♭)
> *Wayfaring Stranger* (E♭)
> *Swing Low, Sweet Chariot* (B♭)
> *Amazing Grace* (D♭)

12-Bar Blues Improvisation

The **12-bar blues** form is so called because it always consists of twelve four-beat measures. Playing the black keys E♭, A♭, and B♭ with your left hand, as illustrated below, begin *Start of the Blues*. The left hand should be playing the given note on every beat. Do not stop or slow down when you change notes—keep the beat moving! If you have trouble doing this at first, try substituting a whole note for the four quarter notes in each bar until you feel confident about the beat.

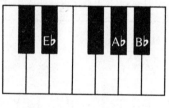

LH

START OF THE BLUES

As soon as you have mastered this left-hand pattern, add the right hand and begin improvising on the black keys. Remember that it is impossible to play a wrong note! Let your right hand move freely on the black keys *and be sure to keep the beat moving.* If at first you have difficulty working with hands together, play various black-key patterns in quarter notes with the right hand (matching the left-hand rhythmic pattern) until you feel comfortable enough to experiment with rhythmic patterns using other note values. Several of these are suggested below to get you started. Try them and then add some of your own.

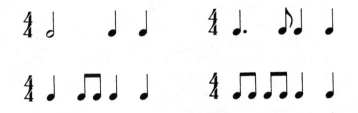

Now that you have worked with the black keys, try improvising in the same manner with just the white keys. Again, all sounds will blend! The pattern of whole steps and half steps formed by the white keys from D to D is the scale of the **Dorian mode.** Following the same procedure described in the paragraph above, practice improvising blues in the Dorian mode. Here is the left-hand pattern:

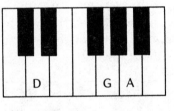

LH

MOVIN' ON THE WHITE KEY BLUES

Improvise five-finger-pattern melodies using the rhythm patterns given below. Improvise a melody using the right hand first, then the left hand, then both hands together. Be sure to end each example on the tonic. Occasional pitches have been provided to give you some help with the melody. Finally, improvise your own five-finger-pattern melodies with rhythms discussed in this unit.

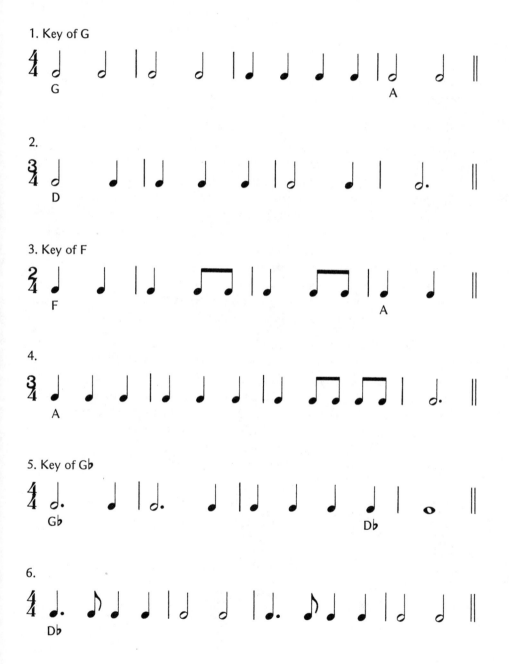

Improvisation with New Notations and Techniques

Some twentieth-century music uses **clusters**, which are sounds constructed of bunched seconds, such as all the tones of a five-finger pattern played simultaneously. Although clusters can be notated traditionally, a new notation consisting of stemmed block-like figures is frequently used. The pitch of a cluster is determined by its position on the staff, as shown below:

blocked clusters
(played simultaneously)

broken clusters
(the notes are played in the direction of the arrow)

Sometimes composers use innovative sounds in their music and invent notations to suit their own purpose. For instance, the tapping of a spoon on a glass might be notated like this: 𝄽 or 𝄽 , or a gradually slowing tempo, like this: ♩♩♩ ♩ ♩ . Frequently the composer will simply give verbal instructions within a specific measure, such as "strike a wooden board," "hum in a high register," and so forth.

Another sound that produces a special effect is the **glissando,** a sweeping sound that is used in both traditional and innovative pieces. This sound is produced by pulling one or more fingernails—usually the nail of the third finger—over the keys. The usual notation is _gliss._

It's Up to You uses the notations we have just discussed. Observe that every measure is in $\frac{4}{4}$, and should be played in strict time, with no change of tempo. Play individual tones, harmonic intervals, clusters, and other sounds according to the written directions and rhythmic patterns provided. For example: ♩ ♩ means to play two half notes, while □ ■ ■ means to play a half-note cluster followed by two quarter-note clusters. Throughout, the exact pitches are up to you!

Following the directions given, improvise using the white keys only the first time you play the piece. Then try improvising with the black keys only. Work with the right or left hand only, then use alternating hands, and finally, try using both hands together wherever possible. You might also try playing this as an improvisational ensemble piece.

IT'S UP TO YOU

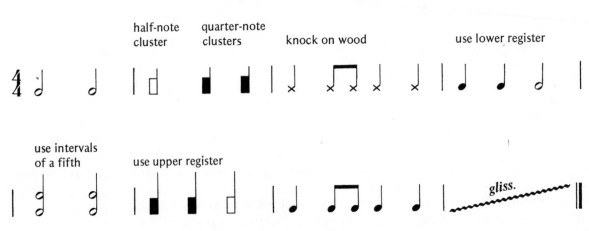

The composers of **aleatoric** (chance) music use the element of chance in creating a piece. For example, pitches and intervals may be determined by the numbers obtained from rolling dice. Aleatoric music also allows the performer to improvise freely or to select an arbitrary arrangement of patterns, as in *Taking a Chance.*

Play the numbered segments of *Taking a Chance* in any order you like. Remember to keep the beat moving! Improvise your own aleatoric segment in the two-measure blank (number 8). Use any of the contemporary techniques discussed so far.

Each time you play *Taking a Chance* it will sound like a different piece.

TAKING A CHANCE

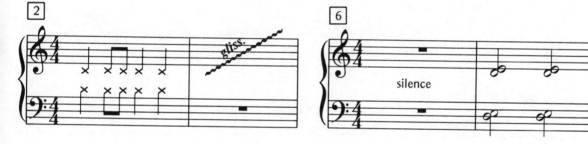

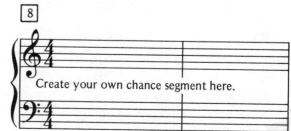

SIGHTREADING STUDIES

1. Name and play the notes in the treble clef with your right hand, using the given fingering. Be sure to look away from the keys. Remember to use the two groups of black keys as reference points to help you locate the correct notes. While you are playing one note be looking ahead in the music to the next one.

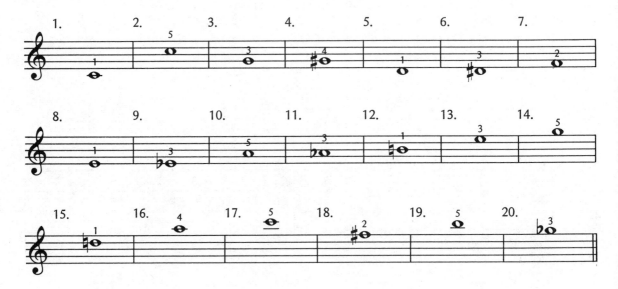

2. Follow the same practice procedure with the left hand as you play the notes below in the bass clef.

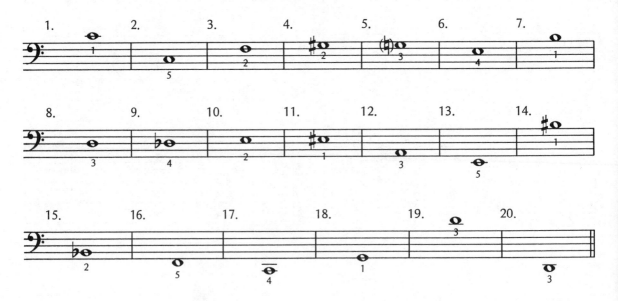

3. For each of the following exercises, place your hand in the correct five-finger position. Do not look at the keys. Do not stop or hesitate to find the notes. Keep the beat moving! Transpose these studies to the various keys studied so far.

1. Key of C

2.

3. Key of G

4.

5. Key of F

6. Key of G♭

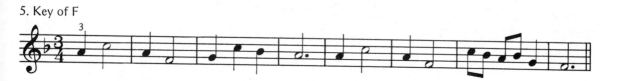

30

7. Key of C

8.

9. Key of G

10.

11. Key of F

12. Key of G♭

ENSEMBLE PIECES FOR FOUR HANDS, TWO PIANOS*

J'AI DU BON TABAC
(I Have Some Good Tobacco)

French (arr. E. M.)

WHISTLE, DAUGHTER

American

*All of these four-hand pieces can be played on one piano if the Piano 1 part is played an octave higher and the Piano 2 part is played an octave lower.

FOLK SONG

French (arr. E. M.)

TAG ALONG

E.M.

MERRILY WE ROLL ALONG

American (arr. E.M.)

ROCK FOR TWO

E.M.

BLACK AND WHITE

Piano 1: White-key clusters—use C-D-E played together.
Piano 2: Black-key clusters—use Gb-Ab-Bb played together.

E.M.

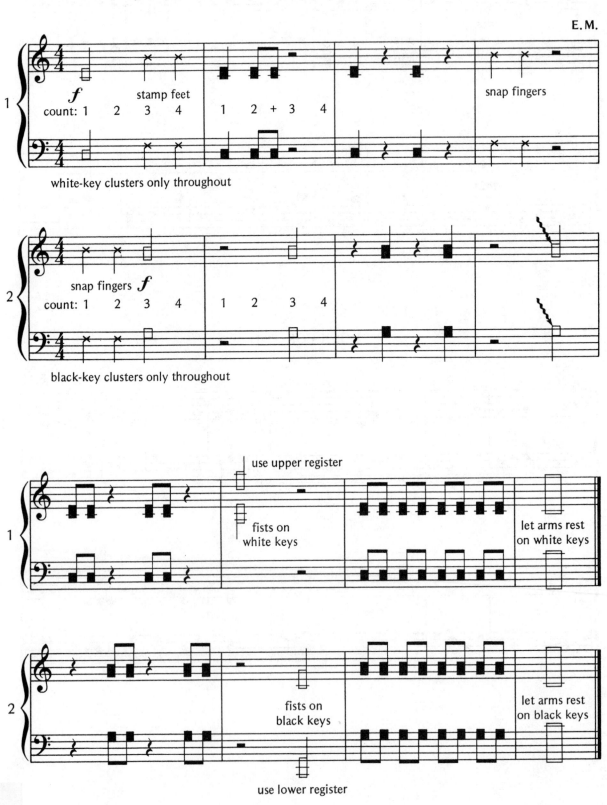

Make sure you understand the following important terms and symbols, which were introduced in this unit. Check the index to find the discussion of any term you need to review. (For definitions of performance terms and symbols, see pages 299-300.)

Keyboard and Notation

register
sharp (♯)
flat (♭)
natural (♮)
five-finger pattern—major
parallel motion
contrary motion
grand staff
treble clef
bass clef
leger line
bar line
measure
double bar line
meter signature—$\frac{2}{4}$, $\frac{3}{4}$, $\frac{4}{4}$ (C)
whole note, whole rest
half note, half rest
quarter note, quarter rest
eighth note, eighth rest
sixteenth note, sixteenth rest

dotted half note
dotted quarter note
tie
beam

Performance

glissando
piano (𝒑)
mezzo piano (𝒎𝒑)
forte (𝒇)
mezzo forte (𝒎𝒇)
legato

Theory

half step
whole step
enharmonic tone
tonic
key

key signature
transposition
melodic interval
harmonic interval
unison
octave
beat
meter
   duple
   triple
   quadruple
rhythm
tempo

Style and Structure

pentatonic scale
twelve-bar blues
Dorian mode
cluster
aleatoric music

2
THE FIVE-FINGER PATTERN

PLAYING IN DIFFERENT REGISTERS

A **register guide** like the one at the beginning of *Walking Up in C* (below) will be used in Units 2 and 3 to help you find the starting note for both hands. It will show the location of middle C, the C an octave higher, and the C an octave lower.

Play the five-finger pattern up the keyboard in C, as shown below. Next transpose the five-finger pattern to other keys of your choice.

WALKING UP IN C

Now play the five-finger pattern down the keyboard, following the above procedure.

WALKING DOWN IN C

Study the rhythmic and melodic patterns of *Little Piece in C.* With the aid of the register guide, find the starting position for both hands.

LITTLE PIECE IN C

Study the interval patterns of thirds which are used in *Study in Skips.*

STUDY IN SKIPS

■ The F♯ in the key signature establishes the key of G, although F♯ does not appear in this piece.

The next two pieces use the same clef for both staffs to avoid the use of a large number of leger lines. Why are the register guides in these two pieces different from the ones previously used?

DEAF WOMAN'S COURTSHIP

■ One flat in the key signature establishes the key of F.

IL ETAIT UN AVOCAT
(He Was a Lawyer)

■ Six flats in the key signature establish the key of G♭.

Alternating Hands

A **canon** is a note-for-note imitation of one melody line by another. *Canon in D* uses alternating hands—first one hand plays, then the other.

Construct the five-finger pattern of D, as shown below:

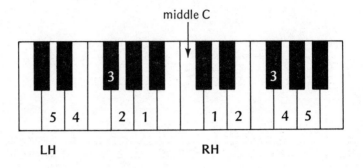

Play *Canon in D* as legato as possible, trying not to look down at the keys as you play. Remember not to sound notes connected by ties. The tied notes in this piece are held for four beats each.

Now try playing this piece in different registers, with the right hand an octave higher than written, the left hand an octave lower.

CANON IN D

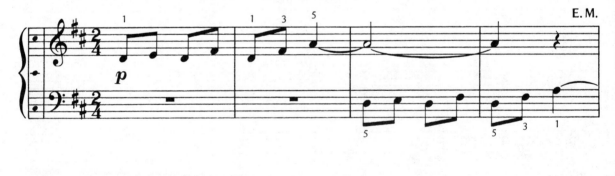

- Find the intervals of a third in this piece.

- A **fermata** (⌢) is used to sustain a note longer than the indicated time value.

- Two sharps in the key signature establish the key of D, although C♯ does not appear in this piece.

When the Saints Come Marching In begins with an **upbeat**, a beat or beats other than the first in the measure, as opposed to a **downbeat** (the first beat). When a piece begins with an upbeat, the missing beats in the first measure will be found at the end of the piece. Here the upbeat consists of three beats, so the last measure consists of one beat.

WHEN THE SAINTS COME MARCHING IN

Traditional

- The repeat sign (:||) indicates that the piece should be repeated from the beginning.

Monday Blues contains accidentals—sharps (♯), flats (♭), and naturals (♮)—which are temporarily added to the body of a piece to alter the pitches (see page 4). Unlike the accidentals in a key signature, these signs are canceled by the bar lines. A natural sign is frequently used as a reminder in the measure following a sharp or flat, as in the right-hand part of bar 2.

MONDAY BLUES

E.M.

Below, *Monday Blues* has been transposed to the key of F, with the left-hand part moved to the lower register. Note the key signature of one flat.

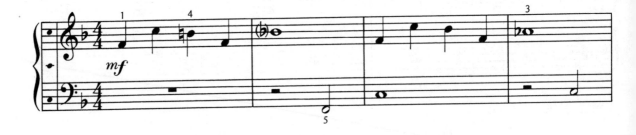

In **parallel motion,** both hands move in the same direction. The left hand in *Some Folks* is playing a harmony to the right-hand melody.

SOME FOLKS

Stephen Foster (1826-1864)

In *Cradle Tune,* both hands are moving in parallel motion with the left hand providing the harmony to the right-hand melody. Before playing the piece, practice the right-hand melody, next the left-hand parallel harmony, and then work with both hands:

Note the curved phrase lines in this piece. A **phrase** is a musical sentence that is usually four or eight measures in length. The end of each phrase is a place of punctuation, and you should lift your fingers off the keys so that there is a slight break (or breathing place) before the next phrase. Be sure you do not interrupt the rhythmic flow of the music when you are phrasing.

Transpose this piece to G and other keys of your choice.

CRADLE TUNE

French
Fine

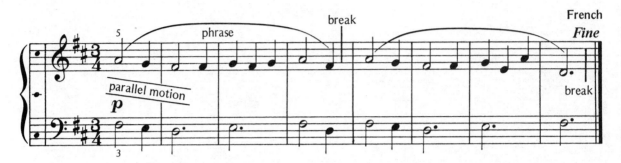

D. C. al Fine

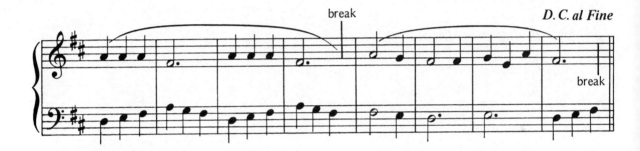

- **Da capo al fine** means to return to the beginning and play to the measure where the word **Fine** (It., "end") appears.

- Find the interval of a fourth in the melody.

The next piece, *Oats, Peas, and Beans,* contains a **sequence**—a pattern of tones that is repeated at a higher or lower pitch. Measures 3 and 4 of this piece have the same tonal pattern as measures 1 and 2, but are played at a higher pitch.

Oats, Peas, and Beans is in ⁶⁄₈ time. In ⁶⁄₈ time there are six beats to the measure, with the *eighth note* receiving the count. Since the eighth note receives one beat, the quarter note has *two* beats and the dotted quarter note *three* beats.

Clap and count aloud the note values for the patterns on the left below. Notice that there is an **accent** (>) on the first and fourth beats in every pattern except the last.

When a piece in ⁶⁄₈ is played quickly, it is easier to count *two* beats to a measure rather than six, with the dotted quarter receiving one beat. Clap and count aloud the patterns on the right below. Accent the first and second beats in every pattern except the last.

How many of these $\frac{6}{8}$ patterns are used in *Oats, Peas, and Beans*?

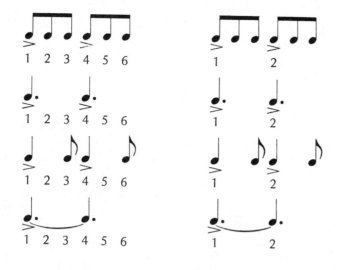

OATS, PEAS, AND BEANS

English

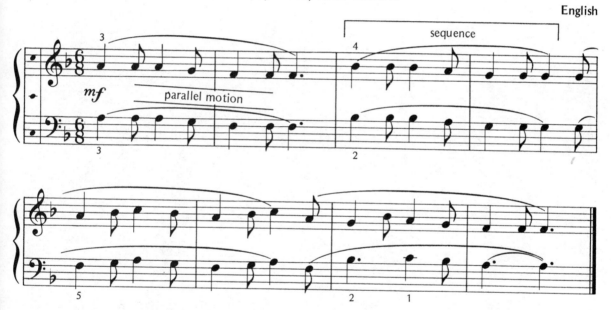

A **slur** is a curved line above or below a combination of two or more notes to indicate that these notes are to be played legato. (Do not confuse this marking with the curved phrase line.) The first note of the slur usually receives more emphasis than the others while the last note of the slur is usually played more softly and is released a bit short of its full note value.

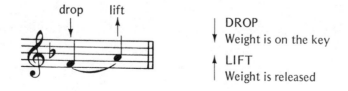

DROP
Weight is on the key

LIFT
Weight is released

Drop the wrist to play the first note of a slur.
Lift the wrist to play the last note of a slur.

46

Practice playing two-note slur combinations of the five-finger patterns ascending and descending first with hands separately, and then with hands together. Then play *Owl* and *Pogo Stick*.

Be sure to observe the difference between the slurs and ties as you play *Owl*.

OWL

John La Montaine (born 1920)

■ The **whole rest** (▬) is used to indicate a full measure of silence in any meter, not just in $\frac{4}{4}$. In *Owl* the value of the whole rest is three beats.

POGO STICK

Moderato

E. M.

- **Staccato** notes are marked with a dot above or below each note. They should be played very crisply and in a detached way. Staccato is the opposite of *legato* (smooth and connected).

- **Moderato** is a tempo marking that means to play at a moderate speed.

Drone Bass

A **drone bass**, an accompaniment that uses the interval of a fifth repeatedly, is effective with many tunes. To construct a drone bass, take the lowest tone (1) and the highest tone (5) of the five-finger pattern you are working in and sound them together with the left hand on the first beat of each measure.

Drink to Me Only with Thine Eyes has a drone-bass accompaniment. It is in the key of A, which has three sharps in the key signature. Construct the five-finger pattern of A, as shown below:

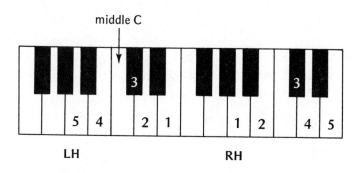

Before playing *Drink to Me Only,* study its rhythmic patterns. Clap the rhythm of the melody while counting the six beats aloud. Next study the melodic pattern. Note the upward or downward direction of movement and the intervals used. Find the intervals of a fifth.

DRINK TO ME ONLY WITH THINE EYES

Moderato   English

eighth-rest

rit.

- The symbol $<$ indicates a gradual increase in loudness. The word **crescendo (cresc.)** means the same thing.

- The symbol $>$ indicates a gradual decrease in loudness. The words **diminuendo (dim. or dimin.)** and **decrescendo (decresc.)** mean the same thing.

- **Ritardando (rit.)** is a word indicating a gradual slowing of the tempo.

Play the same piece in the key of E, which has four sharps in the key signature. Here is the five-finger pattern of E:

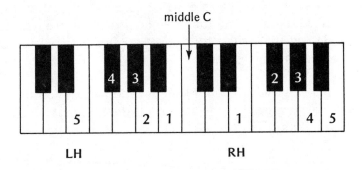

LH   RH

French Tune, which is in the key of E, uses fifths and parallel motion in the left hand to harmonize the melody.

FRENCH TUNE

arr. E. M.

Lento

■ **Lento** is a tempo marking that means to play slowly.

Contrary Motion

In **contrary motion** the hands move in opposite directions. Study the direction of the note patterns in *Reflections* before you play it.

REFLECTIONS

Play the same piece in the key of E♭, which has three flats in the key signature. The five-finger pattern of E♭ is shown below:

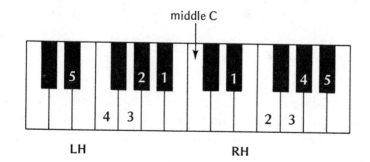

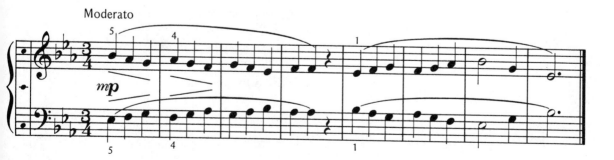

Distant Lands uses contrary motion based on the five-finger pattern of C with an altered second (Db instead of D♮). Before playing the piece, practice the altered five-finger pattern as shown below:

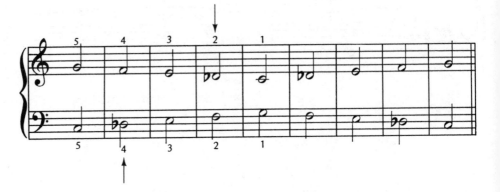

DISTANT LANDS

E.M.

■ **Andante** is a tempo marking that means to play at a walking pace—not too fast, not too slow.

Contrary Motion is in the Dorian mode, using the white keys from D to D. The left hand is in the five-finger position of the Dorian mode, beginning on D, but the right hand is in a new position with the right-hand thumb on G.

Note the change of meter signature in bar 15:

$\dfrac{2}{2}$ ⟨two beats to the measure / the half note receives one beat

$\dfrac{3}{2}$ ⟨three beats to the measure / the half note receives one beat

Keep the same tempo in moving from $\frac{2}{2}$ to $\frac{3}{2}$ and back.

Practice the following five-finger position before playing the piece:

CONTRARY MOTION

Béla Bartók (1881-1945)

Both Parallel and Contrary Motion

Practice the preparatory study below to help you play the next two pieces, which use both parallel and contrary motion.

DUET

Béla Bartók

Moderato

THE FIVE-FINGER PATTERN IN MINOR

To play the five-finger pattern in minor, begin with the five-finger pattern in major and lower the third tone one half step:

Transpose *Erie Canal* to other keys.

Try playing other five-finger melodies such as *Love Somebody* and *Drink To Me Only* in minor by lowering the third tone one half step. Can you hear the difference between major and minor?

ERIE CANAL

W. Allen

Play measures 1, 2, 5, and 6 staccato (detached) and the rest of the piece legato (smooth and connected). Remember that staccato is the opposite of legato.

STUDY IN MINOR

E. M.

IMITATION AND INVERSION

Béla Bartók

- **Imitation** is the repetition of a musical idea in another voice. In **inversion,** a musical idea is presented in contrary motion to its original form.

FIVE-FINGER STUDIES IN MAJOR AND MINOR

Practice the following major and minor five-finger patterns in the keys below. You will be moving up in half steps, or **chromatically,** as you start each five-finger pattern. First, play through all the major five-finger patterns. Next, play the major five-finger pattern followed by the minor pattern, as illustrated. Finally, play just the minor five-finger patterns in all keys.

*The small "m" stands for minor.

TRIADS

A **triad** consists of three tones—the **root**, so called because it is the tone on which the triad is constructed; the **third**; and the **fifth**. A triad is also called a **chord**.

Major triads are formed by taking the first (root), third, and fifth tones of the major five-finger patterns and sounding them together.

Minor triads are formed by taking the first (root), third, and fifth tones of the minor five-finger patterns and sounding them together.

C major chord (I chord)

C minor chord (i* chord)

Triads without their thirds are called **open fifths**. Playing them in half-step progressions is good preparation for playing major and minor triads. Using both hands, construct open fifths starting on C and play them both upward and downward as illustrated below.

Notice that if the lower tone of the fifth is a white key, the upper tone will also be a white key. If the lower tone is black, the upper tone will also be black. The only two exceptions are the fifths B♭-F (black-white) and B-F♯ (white-black).

Open fifths

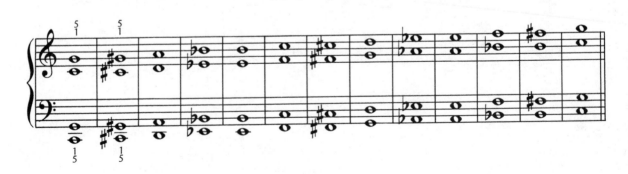

*The small roman numeral denotes a minor chord.

Play the following major and minor triads with each hand separately, then with both hands. Practice playing these chords in various registers.

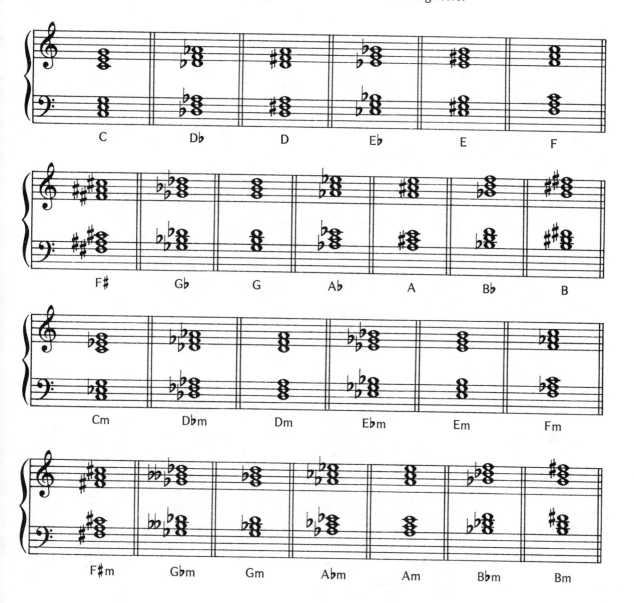

Next play the major-minor-major progression below chromatically upward and downward starting with C. Practice playing these chords in various registers.

etc.

58

Chant uses open fifths in both hands throughout.

CHANT

E.M.

■ **Andantino** is a tempo marking that means somewhat faster than
Andante.

Pyramids uses triads throughout. First name and play the triads without the left-hand part, and then play the piece as written.

PYRAMIDS

E.M.

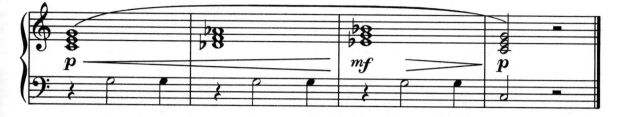

■ An **accent mark** ($\hat{p}$) above or below a note or chord indicates that the note or chord should be stressed.

THE DOMINANT-SEVENTH CHORD

V⁷ (Root Position)

The **V⁷** or **dominant-seventh chord** is constructed by building a major triad on the *fifth* degree of the five-finger pattern in all keys and then adding a minor third.

Five-finger pattern in C

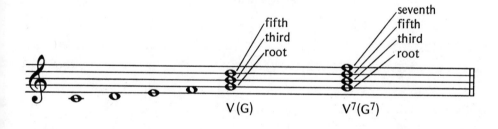

Note that while the V chord has a root, third, and fifth, the V⁷ chord has a root, third, fifth, and seventh.

The roman numeral V represents the fifth degree, the root on which the triad is constructed. The arabic numeral 7, to the right of the V, represents the interval of a seventh between the root and the highest tone of the chord. Since the root is used as the lowest tone of the chord, we say that the chord is in **root position.**

The V⁷ chord also derives its letter name from its root. Thus, in the key of C, as above, the V⁷ chord is called a G⁷ chord; in the key of G, V⁷ is called D⁷; and in D, V⁷ is called A⁷.

The V⁶₅ Inversion

An easier way to play the V⁷ chord is to rearrange, or **invert,** the chord so that a tone other than the root is used as the lowest tone. When the third of the chord is used as the lowest tone, we say that the chord is in **first inversion*** and we call it **V⁶₅**. Note that the root of the chord now appears as the top tone:

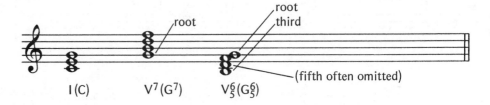

The numbers represent the intervals formed between the lowest tone and the ones above. In V⁶₅ in C, the 6 represents the sixth from B to G, and the 5 represents the fifth from B to F:

Note that V⁶₅ forms its letter name from the fifth degree, the root, just as V⁷ does.

The **V⁶₅ chord** for all keys is constructed by sounding the *fourth* and *fifth* tones of the five-finger pattern together with the tone *a half step down* from the first tone (or *tonic*).

Five-finger pattern in C

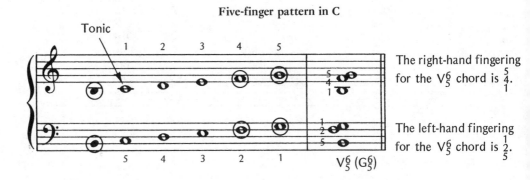

The right-hand fingering for the V⁶₅ chord is 5 4 1.

The left-hand fingering for the V⁶₅ chord is 1 2 5.

When you are playing combinations of I and V⁶₅, remember that the same V⁶₅ chord is used in both major and minor, as illustrated below:

Practice playing I and V⁶₅ chords with the left hand in major and minor in all keys, as shown below. Give the root (or letter name) of each chord as you play it. Remember to look away from the keys. Try to develop a feel for the I—V⁶₅—I progression and anticipate the changing of chords.

*Chords and their inversions are discussed further on page 147.

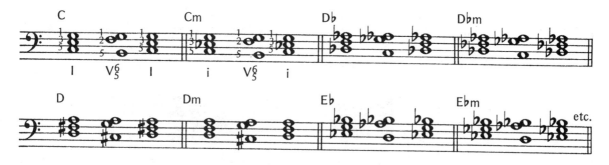

Another way of practicing the I—V$^6_5$—I chord progression is to play the chords with the right hand while the left hand plays the root (or letter name) of each chord as shown below:

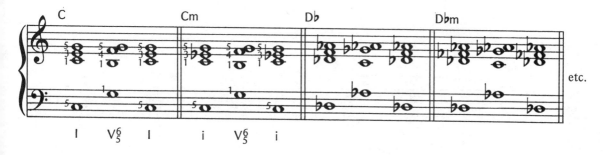

BLOCK-CHORD ACCOMPANIMENTS WITH I AND V$^6_5$

Identify the key of each of the following pieces by checking the key signature. In addition, look at the lowest note at the end of the piece; it will invariably be the tonic, or key note.

Study the rhythmic and melodic patterns of each piece. Play the I—V$^6_5$—I progression several times before trying the two hands together.

Transpose these pieces to other keys.

J'AI DU BON TABAC
(I Have Some Good Tobacco)

Italian Melody appears below in the key of A♭, which has four flats in the key signature. Here is the five-finger pattern:

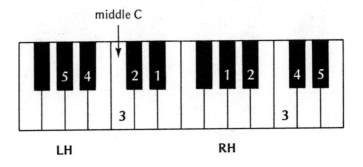

ITALIAN MELODY

LOVE SOMEBODY

■ **Allegretto** is a tempo marking that means to play rather quickly.

Play *Looby Loo* as written; then play it in minor by lowering the third tone in both hands a half step (F♯ becomes F♮).

LOOBY LOO

Allegretto

English

Here we go loo-by loo____ Here we go loo-by light.____

Here we go loo-by loo____ All on a Sa-tur-day night. I

put my right hand in, I take my right hand out, I

give my hand a shake, shake, shake, and turn my-self a-bout.____

THE SUBDOMINANT CHORD

Root Position

The root-position **IV** or **subdominant chord** is constructed by building a major triad on the *fourth* degree of the five-finger pattern in all keys.

Five-finger pattern in C

IV (F)

The IV$_4^6$ Inversion

An easier way to play the subdominant chord is by inverting it to a IV$_4^6$ position, with the *fifth* of the chord as its lowest tone. Note that the root of the IV$_4^6$ chord now appears as the middle tone.

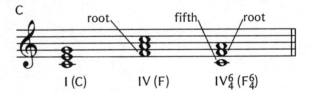

I (C)   IV (F)   IV$_4^6$ (F$_4^6$)

As with V^7 and V$_5^6$, the arabic numbers $_4^6$ represent the intervals formed between the lowest tone and the ones above. In IV$_4^6$ in C, the 6 represents the sixth from C to A, and the 4 represents the fourth from C to F.

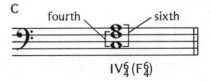

IV$_4^6$ (F$_4^6$)

The **IV$_4^6$** chord for all keys is constructed by sounding the *first* and *fourth* tones of the five-finger pattern together with the *sixth* tone, which is *a whole step up* from the fifth tone of the five-finger pattern.

Five-finger pattern in C

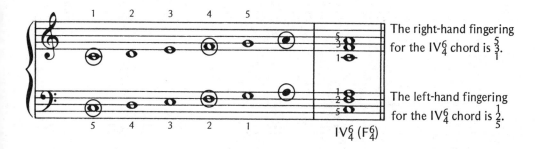

The right-hand fingering for the IV$_4^6$ chord is $\frac{5}{3}$.

The left-hand fingering for the IV$_4^6$ chord is $\frac{1}{2}$.

The IV$_4^6$ chord derives its *letter name* from the root, which is the *fourth* tone of the five-finger pattern. For example, in the key of C, the IV$_4^6$ chord is an F$_4^6$ chord; in the key of G, the IV$_4^6$ chord is a C$_4^6$ chord; and in the key of D, the IV$_4^6$ chord is a G$_4^6$ chord.

Practice playing the chord progression I–IV$_4^6$–I–V$_5^6$–I with the left hand in all major keys, as shown below. Use the fifth tone of the five-finger pattern as the first tone (or **tonic**) of each subsequent chord progression. Remember not to look at the keys. Again, try to develop a feel for the progression and anticipate the changing of chords.

After you have mastered the progression in major keys, try playing the i–iv$_4^6$–V$_5^6$–i progression in various minor keys of your choice. (See the progressions on page 207.) Remember that the i chord in minor has its third lowered a half step, the iv$_4^6$ chord has the sixth tone lowered a half step, but the V$_5^6$ chord remains unchanged.

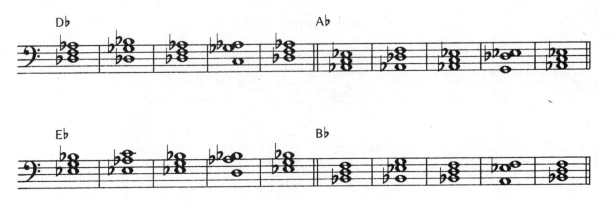

Another way of practicing the I—IV$^6_4$—I—V$^6_5$—I chord progression is to play the chords with the right hand while the left hand plays the root (or letter name) of each chord as shown below:

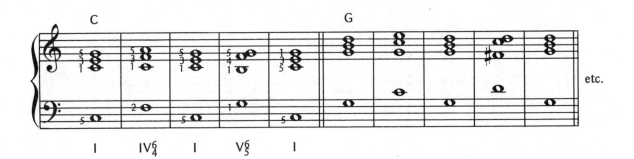

After you have mastered the progression in major keys, try playing the i—iv$^6_4$—i—V$^6_5$—i progression in various minor keys of your choice following the format above.

THE CIRCLE OF FIFTHS AND MAJOR KEY SIGNATURES

When you used the fifth tone of the five-finger pattern in one key to form the first tone of the five-finger pattern in another key, you were constructing what is called the **circle of fifths**:

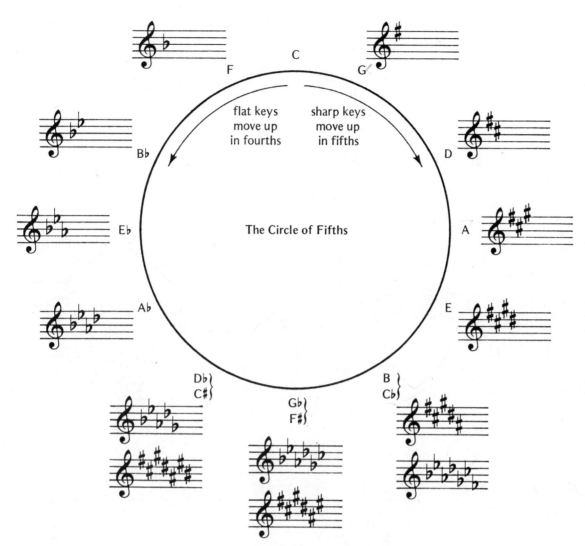

The Circle of Fifths

The circle of fifths is a convenient tool for memorizing key signatures. Read it clockwise for the **sharp keys.** Starting from C and moving by fifths, each new key adds one more sharp to the key signature.

Read it counterclockwise for the **flat keys.** Starting from C and moving by fourths, each new key adds one more flat. Note the enharmonic keys at 5:00, 6:00, and 7:00.

Learn the key signatures of every major key as quickly as possible, either by their order in the circle of fifths, or by remembering this rule of thumb: *the number of sharps and flats in two keys with the same letter names will always add up to seven.* For example:

keys	sharps/flats		total
C, C♯	0, 7		7
G, G♭	1	6	7
D, D♭	2	5	7
A, A♭	3	4	7
E, E♭	4	3	7
etc.			

Remember also that the order of flat keys is just the reverse of the order of sharp keys:

sharp keys: (C) G D A E B F♯ C♯
flat keys: (C) F B♭ E♭ A♭ D♭ G♭ C♭

PIECES WITH I–IV$_4^6$–V$_5^6$ ACCOMPANIMENTS

LITTLE WILLIE

Play *Little Willie* in the key of D♭, as below. Here is the five-finger pattern:

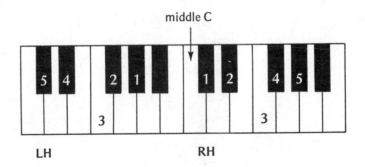

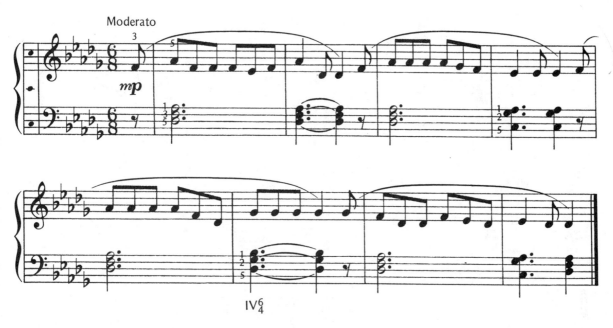

Play *Jingle Bells* in the key of F, as below. Then transpose it to the
key of D♭ and other keys of your choice.

JINGLE BELLS

J. S. Pierpont

MELODY (Op. 39)

Dmitri Kabalevsky

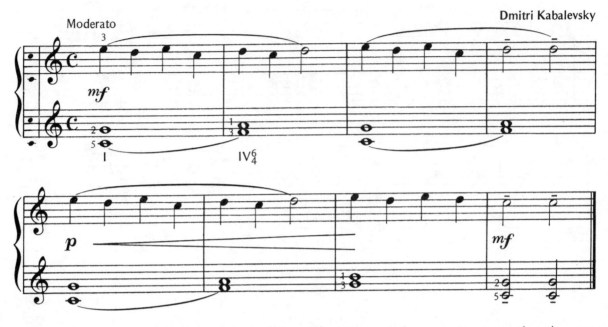

- A short horizontal line (p̄) above or below a note means that the note should be played with a slight accent, thereby sustaining the tone.

Swaying is written in **composite meter**, which is a combination of two different meters. Here $\frac{3}{4}$ and $\frac{2}{4}$ are combined to produce $\frac{5}{4}$.

SWAYING

Irene Harrington Young

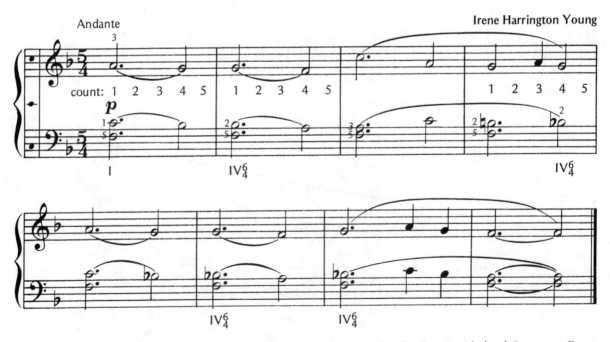

From *Next Door Neighbors*, copyright © 1962 by Summy-Birchard Company, Evanston, Illinois. All rights reserved. Used by permission.

Dance in Miniature is in the key of B♭; here is the five-finger pattern:

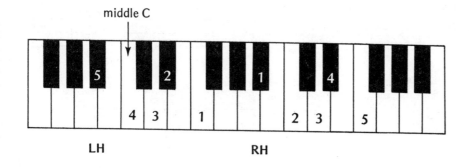

middle C

LH   RH

DANCE IN MINIATURE

Allegro

Dutch

mf

f

- **Allegro** is a tempo marking that indicates a lively, quick pace.

A Winter's Tale is in the key of B; here is the five-finger pattern:

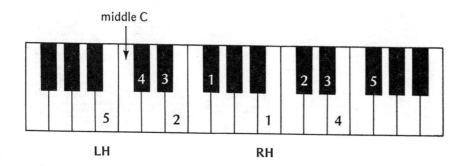

middle C

LH   RH

A WINTER'S TALE

Andante   German

CHANGING FIVE-FINGER POSITIONS

Changing five-finger positions involves moving from one five-finger position to another. This means that you will be shifting the entire hand to a new position.

Practice playing a series of five-finger patterns in various positions. Try to move from one pattern to another without any hesitation in the beat.

Lullaby begins in the five-finger pattern of C, shifts to the five-finger pattern of G, and then returns to the original pattern of C. In measure 4, use the G in both hands as a **pivot tone** to shift to the five-finger pattern of G. Only a fingering change will be required. Try not to look down at the keys when making the change and be sure to keep the beat moving— don't slow down! Use the same procedure when returning to the original position of C.

Except for the examples in the improvisation section of this unit, all hand-position shifts will be indicated by circling the fingerings involved. Practice the hand-position shift below before playing *Lullaby*, and use the same procedure with the pieces that follow.

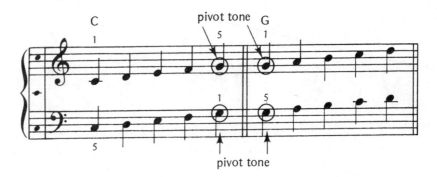

LULLABY

■ **Pianissimo** (*pp*) is a dynamic marking that means to play very softly.

Practice this hand-position shift before playing *Study* by Béla Bartók:

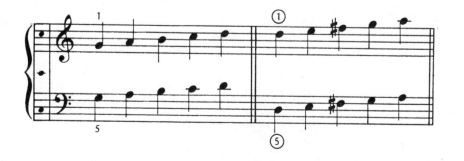

STUDY

Béla Bartók

In *A Little Joke,* both hands are moving in parallel motion, shifting from one five-finger pattern to another. Notice that each five-finger pattern begins one tone lower than the one preceding and that only the white keys are used. Before playing the piece, practice the triads formed by the various five-finger patterns, first with each hand separately and then with both hands:

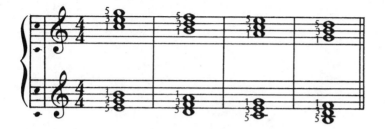

When you play the piece itself, be sure to observe all slur and staccato markings.

A LITTLE JOKE

Dmitri Kabalevsky

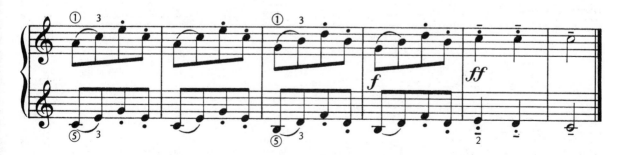

- **Scherzando** means to play in a joking manner, playfully.
- **Fortissimo** (**$f\!f$**) is a dynamic marking that means to play very loud.

Practice this hand-position shift before playing *Steamroller Rock:*

STEAMROLLER ROCK

E. M.

Practice these three hand-position shifts before playing *Time-Clock Blues*. Remember to look ahead of what you are playing to prepare for the hand-position changes.

TIME-CLOCK BLUES

Moderato

E.M.

IMPROVISATION

Pentatonic Improvisation

Using the pentatonic scale (the five black keys), improvise various melodies with the right hand, while using the left hand to play an accompaniment in fifths. The four sets of fifths that can be played on the black keys are shown below:

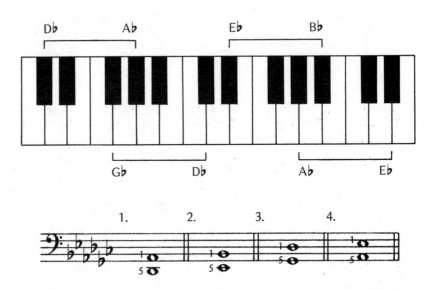

For an "Oriental" sound, play sustained open fifths in the accompaniment, as illustrated in *Hong Kong Walk*. Try playing this piece in different registers—with the right hand one and two octaves higher than written, for example. Finally, try making up your own melody to the accompaniment. At first you might want to retain the same rhythm in the melody, but as you begin to feel at ease, you should then begin to experiment with new melodies, rhythms, accompaniments, and meter groupings.

Remember to keep the beat moving!

Place the right-hand thumb on G♭ and the rest of the fingers on the corresponding black keys:

HONG KONG WALK

Karen Kowalski Thoss

For an "Indian" sound, play a fifth (for example, E♭ and B♭) in the lower register on every beat in $\frac{4}{4}$ meter, as in *Tepee Talk*. With the right hand, begin picking out various melodies on the black keys. Play *Tepee Talk* to give yourself some ideas and then begin to improvise your own melodies.

Place the right hand thumb on D♭ and the rest of the fingers on the corresponding black keys:

TEPEE TALK

Improvise your own accompaniment (single notes, fifths, etc.) on the black keys to the two pentatonic melodies below. Try playing the melody and accompaniment in different registers.

SAPPORO SUNSET

PEACE PIPE

E.M.

12-Bar Blues Improvisation

Before playing *Starting the Blues*, practice the major chords of C, F, and G with your left hand, as shown below. Note that you will have to move the left hand out of position to build these three chords. Start by picking out the tones of C, F, and G with the little finger of your left hand until you can play them easily without looking down at the keys. Work to develop a feel for the distances, or intervals, from one tone to the next. Next practice the chords in the same manner, first as a whole note on the first beat of each measure, and then in the quarter-note figures as written.

STARTING THE BLUES

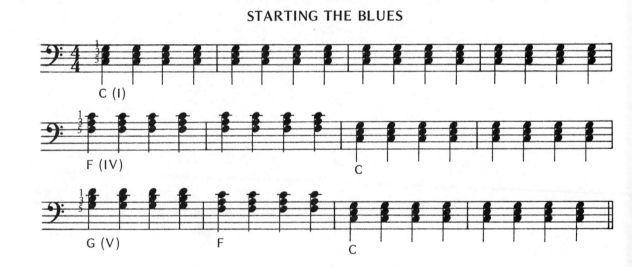

Starting the Blues, like any 12-bar blues, can be played in any major key, using the chords, I, IV, and V. The left hand will always follow this pattern:

4 measures of I
2 measures of IV
2 measures of I
1 measure of V
1 measure of IV
2 measures of I

Playing the major chords of C, F, and G in the left hand, improvise a right-hand melody using the tones in the chord you are playing. For example, with the C chord, the right hand would play a melody with the tones C-E-G; with the F chord, a melody with the tones F-A-C, and so on. Here is a simple example:

Now play *Jump Blues* using the arrangement of C, F, and G chords in both hands. You may want to play quarter-note chords in the left hand as well as whole-note chords. Notice that the same melody pattern is used for each chord and repeated throughout. After playing *Jump Blues,* begin improvising your own melodies using this procedure.

JUMP BLUES

C (I)

F (IV)   C

G (V)   F   C

All kinds of blues melodies can be improvised by changing the note combinations around and using a variety of rhythm patterns. Here are just a few ways of playing the same melody with four different rhythm patterns:

You can improvise melodies not only with the tones in the chord you are playing, but also with all the tones of the *five-finger pattern* for that chord. For instance, in *Walkin' Through Blues* the C-chord melody tones use the five-finger pattern of C, the F-chord melody tones use the five-finger pattern of F (making it necessary to play B♭), and the G-chord melody tones use the five-finger pattern of G. Just remember to match the five-finger pattern to the chord you are playing. In other words, think of the left-hand chord as the key you are playing in when improvising the right-hand melody combinations.

Try improvising different rhythm patterns to the left hand such as

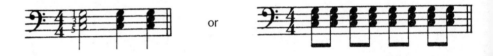

WALKIN' THROUGH BLUES

Now try including what is called the "blue" note. With the right hand, construct the C major chord. Next lower the third a half step from E to E♭ to form a C minor chord. The lowered third, E♭ in this case, becomes the so-called blue note.

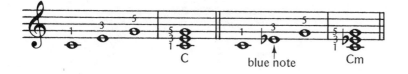

You will be using the three tones of the major chord and also the blue note in *Blue-Note Stomp*. Before playing the piece, practice the individual chord patterns as illustrated below. Use the second finger of the right hand to play the blue note.

BLUE-NOTE STOMP

Try reversing the parts so that the right hand plays the chords, one octave higher, and the left hand plays the melody, one octave lower.

84

Next, for added harmonic color, try improvising melodies to an accompaniment of open fifths that move downward chromatically in several places:

After you are familiar with the downward pattern, try playing fifths that move chromatically *upward* to the fifths on C, F, and G:

Finally, make up your own combinations of fifths moving both downward and upward chromatically to the fifths on C, F, and G, similar to those used in *Blues Beat*.

BLUES BEAT

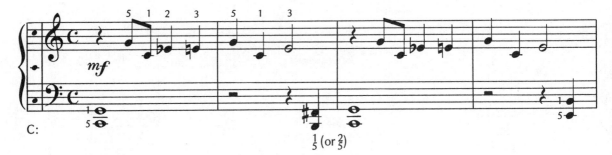

The following accompaniment quite effectively provides the strong, recurring rhythms characteristic of rock music. It uses a broken major triad and a lowered third (blue note):

After practicing this accompaniment pattern, play *Rockin' Blues*. Then, using the same pattern, improvise your own melodies.

ROCKIN' BLUES

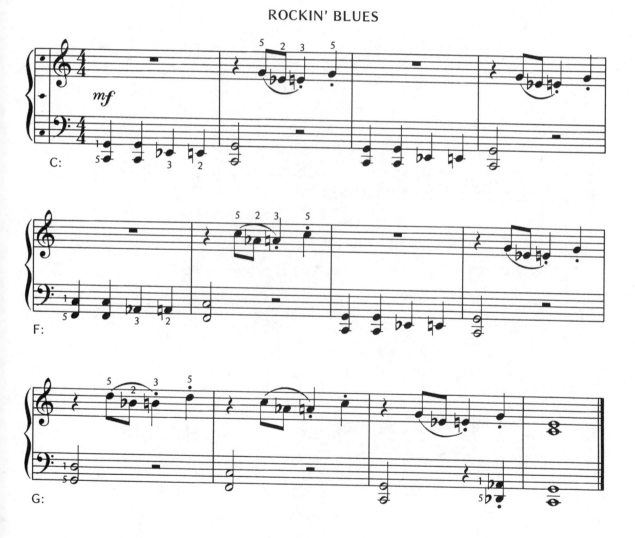

Improvise your own 12-bar blues and transpose to various keys. The following illustrates the I, IV, and V chords in every major key. Use this chart to help work out transpositions in the keys you choose.

I, IV, and V chords for blues improvisation

CREATIVE MUSIC AND HARMONIZATION

The following examples of phrase pairs are designed to help you create music of your own. Each example consists of two matching phrases, each four measures in length. After you have studied and played them, try improvising a matching phrase 2 to the three incomplete examples on page 88.

1. Parallel phrases

In phrase 2 of the first example, measures 5 and 6 are **parallel** to the first two measures of phrase 1, that is, they repeat those measures. Measure 7 uses a change of rhythm and moves stepwise toward the tonic or key note in measure 8.

2. Inverted phrases

In phrase 2 of the second example, measures 5 and 6 repeat the first two measures, but they **invert** (reverse) the order of D-F#-A to read A-F#-D. The rhythmic structure of phrase 2 is identical to that of phrase 1. Measure 7 prepares to move to the tonic with a 4—3—2—3 pattern.

3. Sequential phrases

In phrase 2 of the third example, measures 5 and 6 appear in **sequence** to measures 1 and 2, that is, the same melodic pattern is repeated at a different pitch. As in the first example, measure 7 introduces a change of rhythm (dotted quarter and eighth). Frequent use of the I-chord tones (F, A, C) gives a strong sense of key. Measure 8 ends on the tonic.

Using parallelism, inversion, or sequence, write a phrase that matches each of the three following phrases.

Improvise matching phrases to the five-finger melody given below. Select your best one and write it down for both hands to play. Transpose to other keys. Try playing with the right hand an octave higher, then with the left hand an octave higher. Finally, try playing with both hands in different registers at the same time.

I and V⁶₅ Chords in Major

Harmonize the following melodies with a I or V⁶₅ chord on the first beat of each measure. The right chord will be the one that has some of its tones represented in the melody. Let your ear guide your selection. Write in the chord for each measure.

1.

2.

Write a matching phrase for the phrase below and harmonize using I and V⁶₅ chords.

Add a matching phrase to the phrase below, using a single-note accompaniment in the left hand consisting of tones taken from the I and V⁶₅ chords.

Improvise melodies to the two sets of chords below. Transpose these melodies to as many different keys as possible.

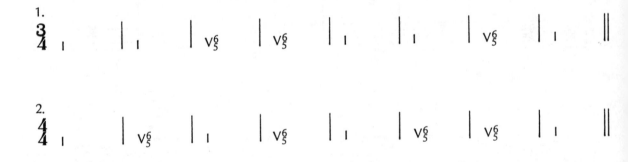

Improvise melodies in major to the chords below using the rhythm patterns given.

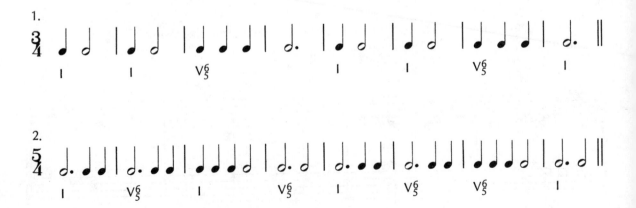

Harmonize the following melody in minor with a i or V$_5^6$ chord on the first beat of each measure. Note that two chords are needed in measure 8.

Improvise matching phrases to the one below, harmonizing the minor melodies with i and V$_5^6$ chords. Then select one melody to write down, including the harmonization.

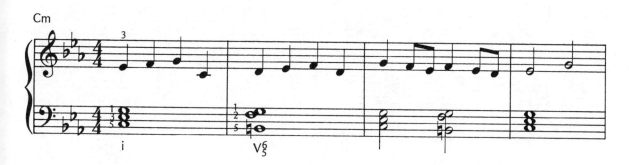

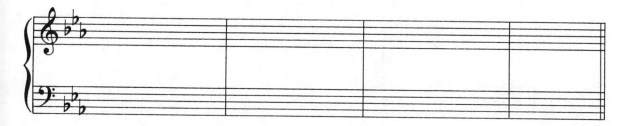

Improvise melodies in minor to the chords given below.

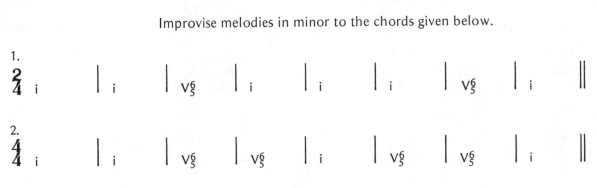

Improvise melodies in minor to the chords below using the rhythm patterns given.

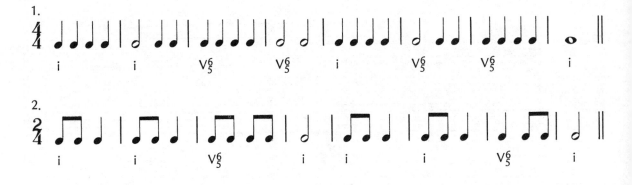

I, IV$_4^6$, and V$_5^6$ Chords in Major

Finish harmonizing the examples below, using I, IV$_4^6$, and V$_5^6$ chords.

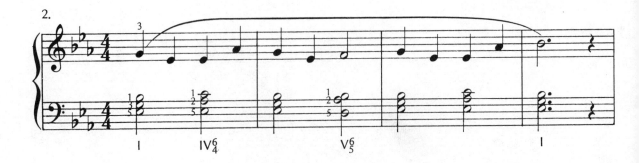

Improvise matching phrases to the one below, using I, IV$^6_4$, and V$^6_5$ chords for the harmonization. Then select one melody to write down, including the harmonization.

1.

Write a melody that blends with the left-hand accompaniment below:

2.

Write two matching four-bar phrases of your own, using I, IV$^6_4$, and V$^6_5$ chords for the harmonization. Select a key and meter signature and don't compose anything you can't play yourself! Try transposing your example to other keys of your choice.

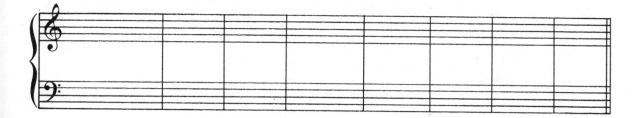

94

Improvise melodies to the chords given below:

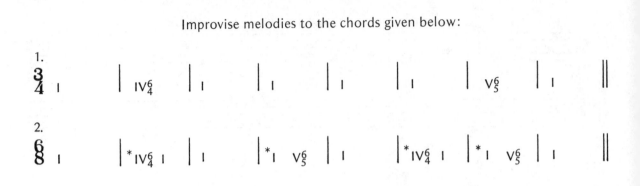

Improvise melodies in major to the chords below using the rhythm patterns given.

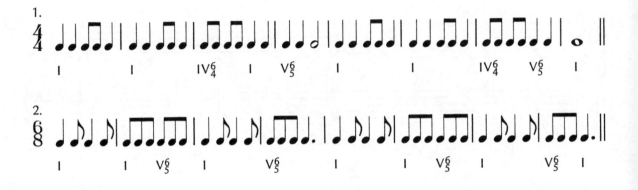

Drone Bass

Improvise melodies in the Dorian mode to the left-hand accompaniment of open fifths.

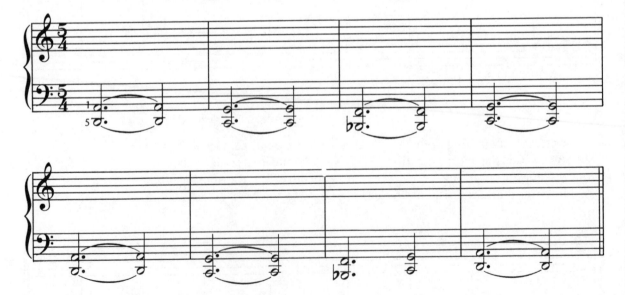

*Use chords on the first and fourth beats of the measure.

Improvise interesting-sounding major and minor triads in the right hand with the accompaniment below:

SIGHTREADING STUDIES

Place hands in the correct position. Be sure not to look at the keys. Do not stop or hesitate to find the notes. Keep the beat moving! You can help yourself maintain an even beat if you select a tempo that allows you to study the music ahead of what you are playing. Transpose these studies to various keys.

Melodies with Various Rhythmic Patterns

1. Key of C

2. Key of G

3. Key of D

4. Key of F

5. Key of A

6. Key of Dm

7. Key of ___

Different Registers and Register Changes

1. Key of ___

2. Key of Gm

3. Key of ____

Slurred Notes

1. Key of G

2. Key of ____

Staccato Notes

1. Key of D♭

Parallel and Contrary Motion

1. Key of A

2. Key of B♭

3. Key of E

Melody with Accompaniment in Fifths

Key of Em

I and V$\frac{6}{5}$ Chords

1. Key of ____

2. Key of Cm

I, IV$\frac{6}{4}$, and V$\frac{6}{5}$ Chords

1. Key of ____

2. Key of E♭

Change of Five-Finger Position

1. Key of G

2. Key of A♭

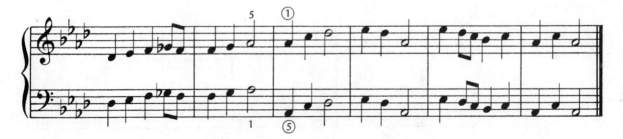

Major and Minor Triads

104

ENSEMBLE PIECES

Four Hands, One Piano

QUAND J'ÉTAIS CHEZ MON PERE
(When I Was at My Father's)

French (arr. E. M.)

NAVY BLUES

- When the octave sign *8va* appears below a note or chord, play it an octave lower than written. When *8va* appears above a note or chord, play it an octave higher than written.

Four Hands, Two Pianos*

THEME from the NEW WORLD SYMPHONY

Antonin Dvořák (1841–1904) (arr. E. M.)

Slowly

*Both these pieces may be played with four hands at one piano if the Piano 1 part is played an octave higher than written and the Piano 2 part is played an octave lower than written. (Much more effective with two pianos, however!)

Six Hands, Three Pianos*

ALOUETTE

French (arr. E. M.)

*Piano 3 is optional. The Piano 1 and 2 parts may be played at one piano if the Piano 1 part is
played an octave higher than written and Piano 2 an octave lower than written.

DRINK TO ME ONLY WITH THINE EYES

English (arr. E. M.)

REVIEW OF TERMS AND SYMBOLS

Make sure you understand the following important terms and symbols, which were introduced in this unit. Check the index to find the discussion of any term you need to review.

Keyboard and Notation

accidentals
slur
five-finger pattern—minor
meter signature—$\frac{6}{8}$

Performance

repeat bar (:‖)
da capo al fine
staccato ( )
accent
Moderato
Lento
Andante
Andantino
Allegretto
Allegro
scherzando

crescendo, cresc. ($<$)
diminuendo, dim. ($>$)
ritardando (rit.)
fortissimo (*ff*)
pianissimo (*pp*)
8va - - - - - - - -

Theory

chromatic
major triad
minor triad
pivot tone
dominant-seventh chord
    (V^7 and V^6_5)
subdominant chord (IV and
    IV^6_4)
root
root position
inverted chord
circle of fifths

sharp keys
flat keys
compound meter
composite meter

Style and Structure

canon
imitation
parallel motion
contrary motion
upbeat
downbeat
sequence
phrase
    parallel
    inverted
    sequential
drone bass
open fifth
"blue" note

PIECES WITH EASY ACCOMPANIMENTS

3

This unit introduces pieces that go beyond the five-finger pattern—that is, pieces with an extended range—along with a variety of easy accompaniments to play and improvise.

Most melodies and chords are based on some kind of scale system. A **scale** (from the Italian word *scala,* ladder) is a step-by-step series of tones in a specific pattern. In most scales, this pattern is a combination of whole steps and half steps.

In the **major scale,** the pattern consists of eight tones with half steps between tones 3 and 4 and between 7 and 8, and with whole steps between the other tones. All major scales adhere to this pattern:

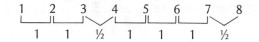

In the C major scale, the half steps occur between E and F and between B and C:

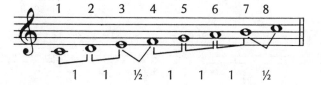

In all other major scales, it is necessary to use one or more black keys (accidentals) to preserve the pattern of whole steps and half steps:

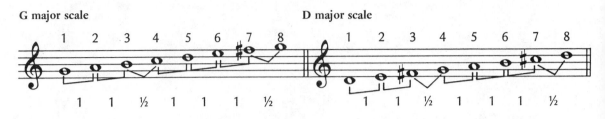

The major scales and their key signatures are shown in the following list. Each **sharp scale** begins on the fifth degree of the preceding scale (the clockwise order of the circle of fifths, page 67). Each new scale retains the sharp or sharps of the previous scale and adds one new sharp to the seventh degree. Each **flat scale** begins on the fourth degree of the preceding scale (the counterclockwise order of the circle of fifths). Each new scale retains the flat or flats of the previous scale and adds one new flat to the fourth degree.

Practice playing these scales, first with hands separately, then with hands together. Be sure to observe the fingerings provided. The five-finger pattern of any key is taken from the first five tones of the corresponding scale. Only the fingerings differ.

Major scales and fingerings

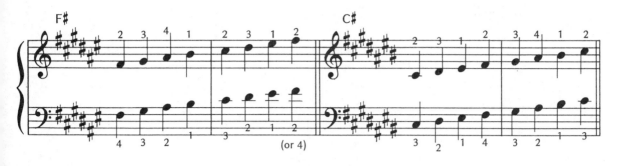

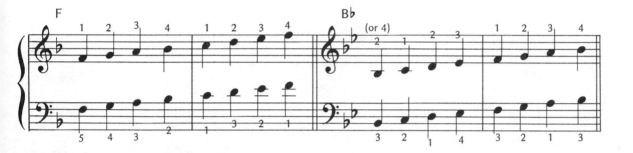

SCALE STUDIES IN CLUSTERS

The major scales can be practiced in clusters to learn the scale pattern and their specific fingerings more easily. With one hand at a time, block scales as illustrated below, moving from one group to the next in a continuous motion.

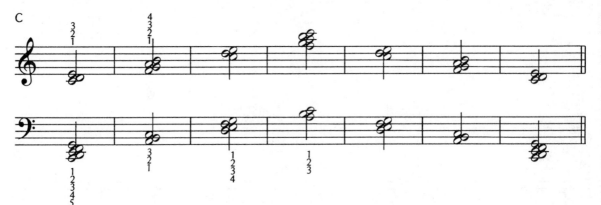

The black-key scales—B (Cb), C♯ (Db), and F♯ (Gb)—can be learned more readily when they are blocked. These black-key scales that follow should be practiced both ascending and descending, first with hands separately, and then with both hands together.

Note that each hand uses the same fingering:

| the group of two black keys | R.H. | 2-3 |
| | L.H. | 3-2 |

| the group of three black keys | R.H. | 2-3-4 |
| | L.H. | 4-3-2 |

the white keys use thumbs of each hand

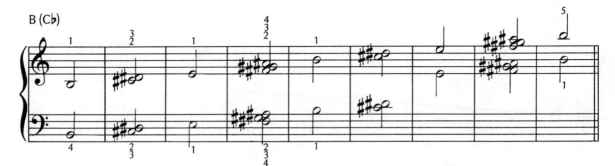

F# (Gb)

TRIADS ON MAJOR-SCALE DEGREES

Triads, like other chords, can be constructed on every degree (tone) of the scale of any key, taking into account the sharps or flats in the key signature for that key. Triads constructed on the first, fourth, and fifth degrees are *major*. Triads constructed on the second, third, and sixth degrees are *minor*. The triad constructed on the seventh tone is *diminished* (see page 256).

C major

Scale degree:	Tonic	Supertonic	Mediant	Subdominant	Dominant	Submediant	Leading tone
Letter name:	C major	D minor	E minor	F major	G major	A minor	B diminished
Roman numeral:	I	ii	iii	IV	V	vi	vii°

Each triad can be identified by its scale-degree name, its letter-name chord symbol, or the roman numeral traditionally used to designate the scale degree. Large roman numerals are used for major triads, small roman numerals for minor triads.

To identify triads and other chords by scale-degree names or roman numerals, you must know the key of a piece. For example, if asked to play a dominant (V) chord, you would play a G major triad in the key of C, and an A major triad in the key of D.

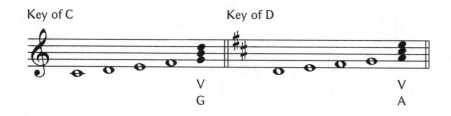

Key of C ... V / G   Key of D ... V / A

Play triads on each scale degree in the keys of C, F, and G. As you play the chord, give the scale degree and identify the chord by letter name.

EXTENDING THE FIVE-FINGER POSITION

Melodies that extend beyond the five-finger position have certain fingering changes that differ from the fingerings of the five-finger position. Most of these changes will be one of the following four types:

1. **Extension:** The fingers extend outside the five-finger position.

2. **Substitution:** The fingers are changed on the repeat of the same tone or tones.

3. **Contraction:** The fingers are contracted (brought closer together) within the five-finger position.

4. **Crossing:** The finger or fingers cross over or under another finger or fingers.

Throughout this unit and the next, fingering numbers that use any of the four types of fingering change above will be circled.

The song *Lavender's Blue* uses extended fingering in the melody. The fifth finger must move out of the five-finger position to play the interval of a sixth formed by the notes D and B.

LAVENDER'S BLUE

La - ven - der's blue, dil - ly, dil - ly, La - ven - der's green. When I am

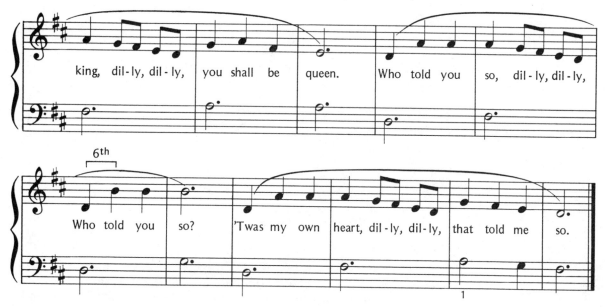

Kum Ba Ya uses extended fingering in the melody.

KUM BA YA

Moderato   **Traditional**

- ¢ (*alla breve*) is a meter signature that indicates **cut time** (²⁄₂), in which each measure has two strong half-note beats.

This Old Man uses sixteenth notes in the melody.

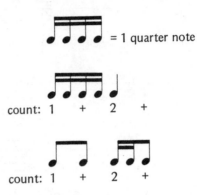

count: 1   +   2   +

count: 1   +   2   +

The fourth finger is used on the first note of the melody so that the fifth finger is available to play the extended melody pattern in bar 3. In bars 4-5, an example of contraction occurs in the right-hand part when the fifth finger moves directly next to the third finger so that the thumb is available to play D.

Remember not to look down at the keys when making fingering changes.

THIS OLD MAN

English

You will find examples of extended fingering in *Oh! Susanna.* The piece includes not only sixteenth notes but a dotted-eighth note followed by a sixteenth note:

count: 1   +   2   +   ah

Another way of practicing this dotted-note rhythm is to count a fast four for the sixteenth-note groupings, with the sixteenth note coming in on four:

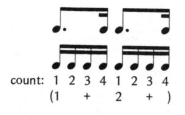

count: 1 2 3 4 1 2 3 4
(1 + 2 +)

OH! SUSANNA

Allegretto

Stephen Foster (1826–1864)

I__ came from Al - a - ba - ma with my ban - jo on my
It__ rained all night the day I left, The wea - ther it was

knee, I'm__ goin' to Loui - si - an - a, My__ true love for to see.
dry, The__ sun so hot I froze to death, Su - san - na, don't you cry.

Oh! Su - san - na, oh, don't you cry for me; For I'm

goin' to Loui - si - an a, My__ true love for to see.

120

Examples of extension and substitution of fingering are found in *Frère Jacques*. Play this piece as a **round,** with each person (or group) starting two measures after the preceding entrance.

FRÈRE JACQUES

French

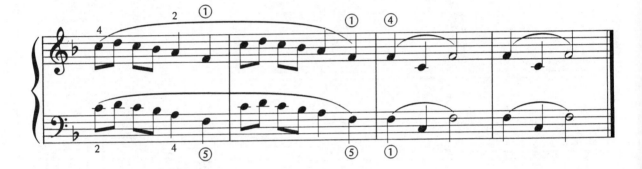

Examples of fingers crossing over and under are found in *Scale Study*.

SCALE STUDY

Carl Czerny (1791-1857)

Tallis's Canon uses crossing, extension, and substitution in both hands. Be sure to observe the correct fingering as you practice.

This canon can be played as a duet with each person (or group) playing a single line, either with one hand or both hands.

TALLIS'S CANON

Thomas Tallis (1505-1585)

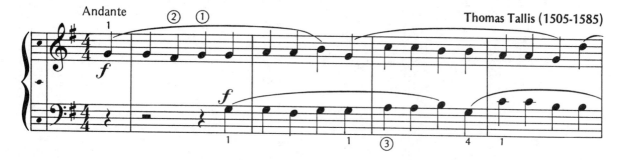

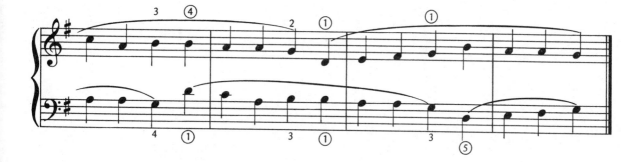

Little Dance has a melody that is largely made up of broken triads (F major, G minor, and G major), with the same triadic figure used in the accompaniment.

With the right hand, practice playing the triads of F major, G minor, and G major, first as block chords and then as arpeggios (broken chords), as illustrated below:

With the left hand, practice the chordal figures below:

When you play the piece, be sure to observe the staccato markings and change of dynamics. Transpose the piece to the key of G.

LITTLE DANCE

Dmitri Kabalevsky

MUSICAL FORMS: AB AND ABA

The word **form** refers to the architecture or structure of music. Two of the most common forms used in songs are **two-part song form** (sometimes referred to as **binary** or **AB form**) and **three-part song form** (sometimes referred to as **ternary** or **ABA form**).

Two-part song form or AB form is illustrated with the song *Yankee Doodle:*

A—phrase 1
A'—variation of phrase 1
B—contrasting phrase (introduces new material)
B'—repeat of contrasting phrase (with some alteration at the end)

The left-hand accompaniment in *Yankee Doodle* uses an open fifth with the addition of a grace note, which is an ornamental note. Grace notes do not receive any specific time value, and they are to be played quickly.

The grace notes in this piece are always a half step down from the top note of the open fifth and should all be played with the second finger. The combination of grace note and open fifth gives a bagpipe effect. Practice the grace notes below, then play *Yankee Doodle*.

YANKEE DOODLE

Three-part song form or ABA form is illustrated with the song *Irish Washerwoman.*

A—phrase 1
A'—repeat of phrase 1 with some alteration
B—contrasting phrase (introduces new material)
A'—phrase 1 and repetition (Da Capo section)

IRISH WASHERWOMAN

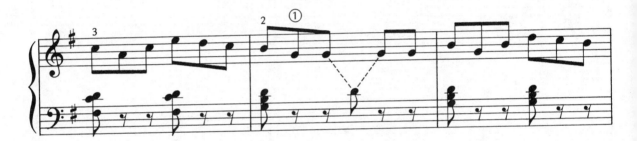

D.C. al Fine

■ **Con moto** is a tempo marking that means to play quickly, "with motion."

BROKEN-CHORD ACCOMPANIMENT PATTERNS

Practice the following broken-chord accompaniment patterns and substitute some of them in the pieces you have learned so far. The patterns use I, IV$^6_4$, and V$^6_5$ chords, and they are in a variety of meters. For simplicity, all are notated in the key of F. Transpose to other keys as necessary.

First, here is the basic pattern in block-chord form:

$\frac{2}{4}$ Pattern

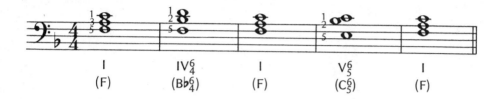

$\frac{3}{4}$ Patterns

$\frac{4}{4}$ Patterns

126

⁶/₈ Patterns

Frankie and Johnny uses a broken-chord pattern in the accompaniment.

FRANKIE AND JOHNNY

Moderato   Traditional

Frank-ie and John-ny were lov-ers, Oh, Lord-y how they could

love. They swore to be true to each oth-er, just as true as the stars a-

bove, He was her man, but he done her wrong.

The next piece, *Du, du liegst mir im Herzen,* uses the **waltz pattern,** a broken-chord accompaniment in which the first beat is stressed and the second and third beats are played as if they were staccato. Think of playing *down* on the key for beat one, and playing *up* on the keys for the other two beats.

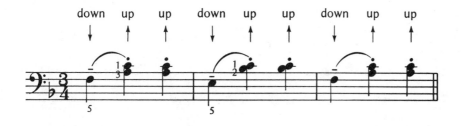

DU, DU LIEGST MIR IM HERZEN
(You Live in My Heart)

ARPEGGIO ACCOMPANIMENT PATTERNS

An arpeggio is a chord in which every note is played separately, one after the other. Practice the following arpeggio patterns in the same way as described on page 125 for broken-chord patterns.

$\frac{2}{4}$ Patterns

$\frac{3}{4}$ Patterns

$\frac{4}{4}$ Patterns

$\frac{6}{8}$ Patterns

In *On Top of Old Smoky*, the left-hand accompaniment is made up of arpeggio figures based on the I, IV_4^6, and V_5^6 chords. Practice playing the left-hand accompaniment as a block chord while you hum the melody. Then break the chords into arpeggios as notated below. Notice that the first four notes of the melody form an arpeggio of the C major chord.

130

ON TOP OF OLD SMOKY

Traditional

Practice the arpeggio accompaniment in *Barcarolle* in the same way that you did for *Old Smoky*.

BARCAROLLE

Jacques Offenbach (1819-1880)

The **Alberti bass** is an accompaniment pattern using a repeated broken-chord figure arranged with the lowest tone first, followed by the highest tone, then the middle tone, then a repeat of the highest tone. It is named after the Baroque composer Domenico Alberti, who frequently used this kind of accompaniment in his music, as did later Classical composers.

The next piece uses an Alberti bass.

AH, VOUS DIRAI-JE, MAMAN?
(Ah, Shall I Tell You, Mama?)

French

■ **Sempre staccato** means "always staccato." Note that staccato dots are unnecessary with this instruction.

SYNCOPATION

Syncopation is a rhythmic effect in which the accents are placed on the off-beats (weak beats) of the measure. In *The Entertainer*, the right-hand melody uses syncopation by placing a longer note value on a weak beat (the second half of beat 1), so that the weak beat is stressed.

count: 1 + 2 + 3   4

This piece has a **first ending** and a **second ending**:

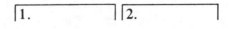

After playing the piece through, go back to the beginning and play it again, this time skipping the first ending and going directly to the second ending.

THE ENTERTAINER

Scott Joplin (1868-1917)

The **damper pedal** is the rightmost pedal on the piano. It is used to obtain more resonance and to connect and sustain tones that require legato playing. This pedal releases the felt dampers from the strings and allows the strings to continue vibrating freely.

Push the pedal down with the right foot, hold as indicated by the markings below, and then release. Remember to keep your heel on the floor while pedaling.

```
L_____⌐
down        up
```

Other standard pedal markings are:

```
down    up-down                    down   up    down   up        down        up
L_____∧_____∧_____∧_____    L___⌐   L___⌐        Ped.        ✳
```

Direct Pedaling

Depress the damper pedal directly with the chord, as indicated by the markings above. As the chord is struck, the pedal is depressed simultaneously. Then the pedal is released on one of the following beats. This type of pedaling is used primarily for resonance and to achieve a stronger feeling of legato. No attempt is made to bind all harmonies together.

Pedal Studies

Using direct pedaling, practice playing triads using the white keys only:

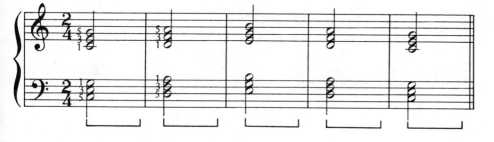

Practice direct pedaling with arpeggio patterns:

The Highlands uses direct pedaling.

THE HIGHLANDS

Play *Wayfaring Stranger*, observing the pedal markings throughout. The whole piece is played on the black keys, and its accompaniment consists entirely of an E♭ minor triad and one variation of that triad, as shown below:

E♭m triad

WAYFARING STRANGER

Andante

Traditional

I'm just a poor___ way-far- ing stran-ger,___ A- trav-'ling through this world of woe;___ But there's no sick - ness, toil nor dan-ger,___ In that bright world to which I go.___ I'm go- ing there___ to see my mo-ther, I'm go- ing there no more to roam.___ I'm just a go- ing o- ver Jor-dan.___ I'm just a go- ing o- ver home.

OSTINATO ACCOMPANIMENT PATTERNS

An **ostinato pattern** is a constantly recurring melodic figure usually found in the bass. *He's Got the Whole World in His Hands* uses an ostinato figure called a **walking bass**. Notice how the four tones of the walking bass move down scalewise, beginning with the root of the appropriate chord:

HE'S GOT THE WHOLE WORLD IN HIS HANDS

Spiritual

The accompaniment pattern in the first section of *Go Tell It on the Mountain* is an alternating figure that uses the I and IV$^6_4$ chords with the middle voice omitted.

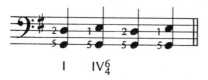

I   IV$^6_4$

GO TELL IT ON THE MOUNTAIN

SECONDARY CHORDS

The **primary chords**, I, IV, and V, have been used in blues improvisation and in a variety of accompaniment patterns so far. The **secondary chords** ii, iii, and vi can also be used to accompany melodic lines. They are often referred to as substitute chords for I, IV, and V.

The ii Chord (Supertonic)

The **ii chord** (supertonic) is a minor triad constructed on the second degree of the major scale. It is sometimes substituted for the IV chord since the chords have two tones in common.

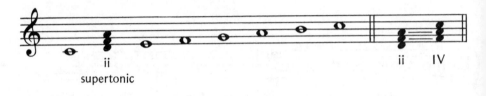

Practice playing the following chord progressions using the ii chord in all major keys, always noting common tones in the movement from one chord to the next.

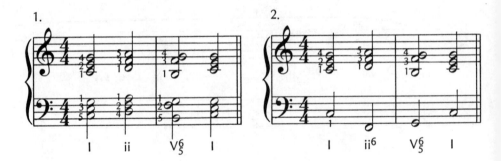

The iii Chord (Mediant)

The **iii chord** (mediant) is a minor triad constructed on the third degree of the major scale. It is sometimes substituted for the V chord since the chords have two tones in common.

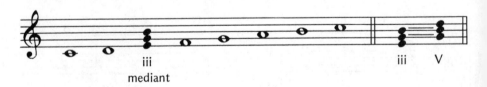

Practice playing the following chord progressions using the iii chord in all major keys, again noting common tones in the movement from one chord to the next.

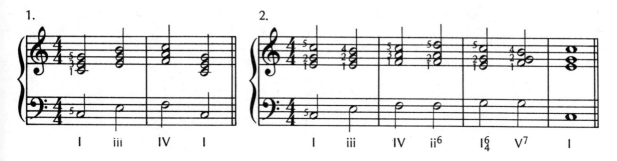

The vi Chord (Submediant)

The vi Chord (Submediant)

The **vi chord (submediant)** is a minor triad constructed on the sixth degree of the major scale. It is sometimes substituted for the I chord since the chords have two tones in common.

Practice playing the following chord progressions using the vi chord in all major keys, again noting common tones in the movement from one chord to the next.

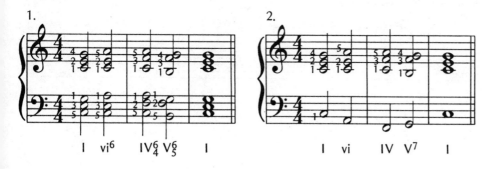

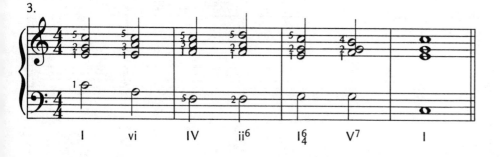

The song *Shenandoah* uses the mediant (iii) and submediant (vi) chords in the accompaniment.

SHENANDOAH

American

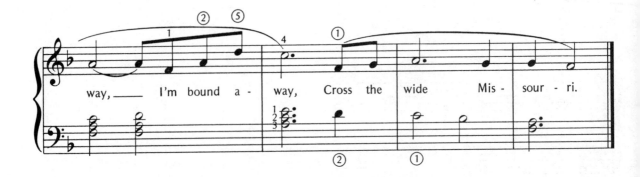

Before playing *Every Night When the Sun Goes Down*, study the triads that make up the accompaniment pattern. Give the letter names (C, Dm, etc.) of the triads used in this piece.

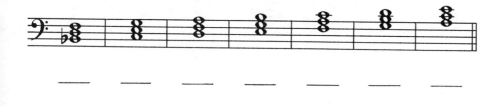

EVERY NIGHT WHEN THE SUN GOES DOWN

Allegretto

American

Oregano Rock uses the supertonic (ii) and mediant (iii) chords in the right-hand part. Practice the triads below as a warm-up for this piece.

OREGANO ROCK

E.M.

INTERVALS WITHIN THE SCALE

The intervals formed between the tonic and the other degrees of the major scale are illustrated below:

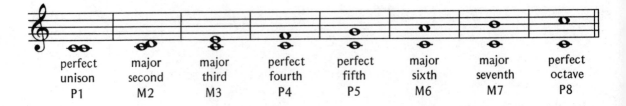

perfect unison	major second	major third	perfect fourth	perfect fifth	major sixth	major seventh	perfect octave
P1	M2	M3	P4	P5	M6	M7	P8

Perfect intervals: unison, fourth, fifth, octave

Major intervals: second, third, sixth, seventh

A **perfect interval** becomes **diminished** when the top tone is lowered a half step, or when the bottom tone is raised a half step.

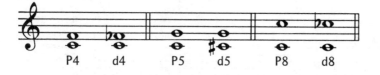

A **major interval** becomes **minor** when the top tone is lowered a half step, or when the bottom tone is raised a half step.

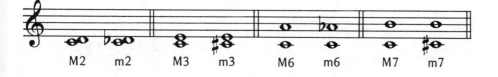

A major or perfect interval becomes **augmented** when the top tone is raised a half step.

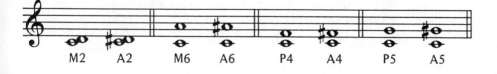

Practice building and playing melodic and harmonic intervals in various major keys of your choice. Name each interval.

MELODIC LINES WITH INTERVALS

Melodies using various intervals harmonically appear on the following pages.

Seconds

The Chase uses harmonic and melodic major seconds (a whole step apart) throughout the right hand:

Notice that the right hand "chases" the left at the distance of a minor second (one half step) throughout.

144

This piece is **bitonal**, which means that it is in two different keys simultaneously. The left hand is pentatonic, using only the five black keys, spelled here with sharps instead of flats. The right hand uses only the white keys in the five-finger pattern of C major.

THE CHASE

Stan Applebaum

Thirds

Practice the following preparatory exercise in thirds before playing *Carol of the Drum.*

CAROL OF THE DRUM

Katherine Davis

rum-pa-pum-pum,_____ "Our new-born King to see! Pa-

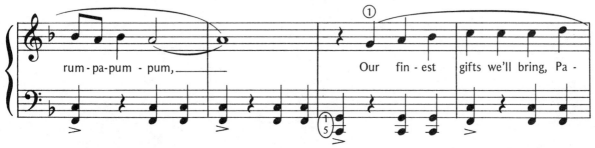

rum-pa-pum-pum,_____ Our fin-est gifts we'll bring, Pa-

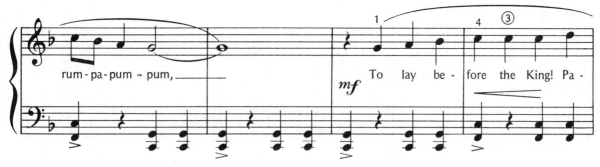

rum-pa-pum-pum,_____ To lay be-fore the King! Pa-

rum-pa-pum-pum, Rum-pa-pum-pum, Rum-pa-pum-pum,_____

So to hon-or Him, Pa-rum-pa-pum-pum,_____

When_ we come."_____

Sixths

Tucky Walk uses sixths throughout as illustrated below:

TUCKY WALK

E.M.

As discussed in Unit 2, a chord is **inverted** when a chord tone other than the root is in the bass.

Triads may be inverted twice. When the third of the chord is in the bass, the chord is in **first inversion**. When the fifth of the chord is in the bass, the chord is in **second inversion.**

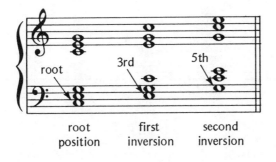

Seventh chords have three inversions:

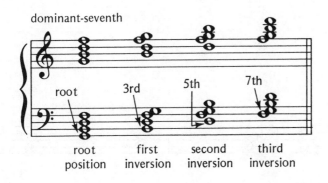

The numbers beneath the chords below represent the intervals that make up the chord, counting up from the bottom note to the notes above. For example, in the first inversion of the C major triad, the C$^6_3$, E to C is an interval of a sixth and E to G is an interval of a third.

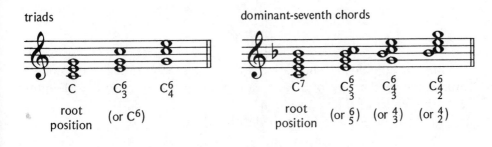

Practice playing chord inversions with correct fingerings in all keys, first with hands separately and then together. The inversions for the C, G, and D chords are given below. Continue in the circle-of-fifths order for the remaining keys.

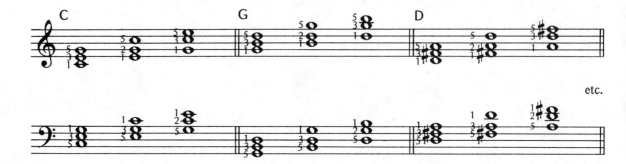

etc.

Identify and play the following major triads using the symbols as illustrated:

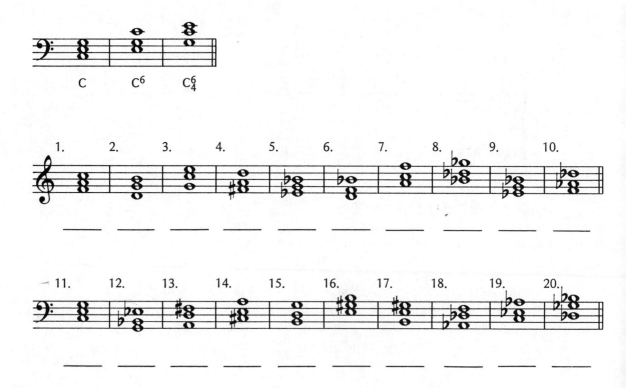

Minuet contains a **modulation**, or change of key. It begins in D minor, modulates to the key of F in measure 13, and then returns to D minor with the repeat of the first section.

Find the inverted triads in the left-hand part.

MINUET

Con moto; grazioso

Leopold Mozart (1719–1787)

D.C. al Fine

■ **Grazioso** means gracefully.

Triads on the Run uses triads in second inversion for the first eight measures, and in first inversion for the last eight measures.

TRIADS ON THE RUN

E.M.

The pentatonic melody in *Pagoda* is harmonized in fourths throughout. Using the right hand, practice the following pattern of fourths, observing the correct fingering.

PAGODA

E.M.

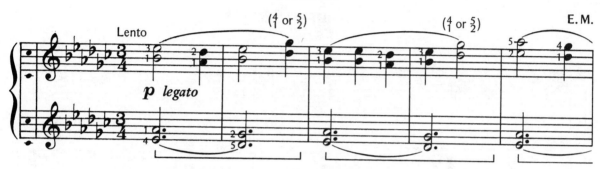

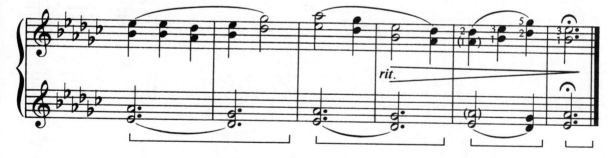

■ **Una corda** ("one string") is the marking for the use of the soft pedal, which is located on the left.

In *Modern Age*, the melodic line and the intervals of a fourth in the accompaniment combine to cause dissonance. **Dissonance** is a combination of tones conventionally accepted as being in a state of unrest and as having a harshness of sound. Practice the following basic patterns for this piece:

The second pattern appears sequentially in measures 5-8 in both hands.

MODERN AGE

Play heavily

Daniel Hooley

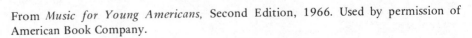

From *Music for Young Americans*, Second Edition, 1966. Used by permission of American Book Company.

Prologue, a contemporary work by Vincent Persichetti, uses major triads in both hands to create an occasional biting dissonance.

PROLOGUE

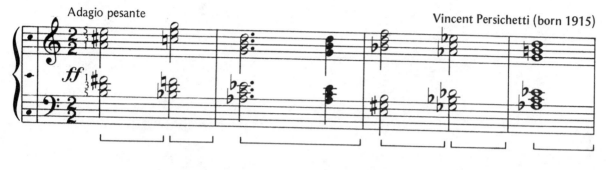

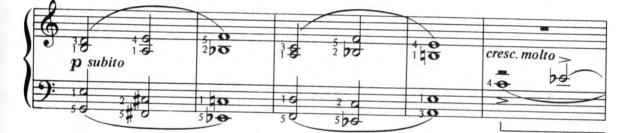

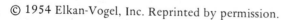

© 1954 Elkan-Vogel, Inc. Reprinted by permission.

THE DAMPER PEDAL 2

Indirect (Legato) Pedaling

Indirect or **legato pedaling** is used to obtain a very smooth connection of tones. Depress the damper pedal *immediately after* sounding the chord. As you play each subsequent chord, release the pedal quickly, then depress it immediately once again.

Pedal Studies

Using indirect pedaling, practice playing triads on the white keys only.

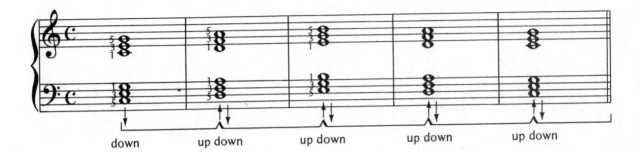

down   up down   up down   up down   up down

Practice the following two chord progressions in various keys.

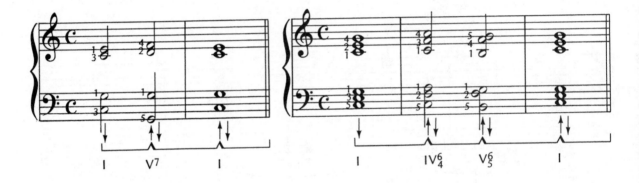

The right-hand part of *Big Ben* uses inverted triads throughout. Be sure to observe the legato pedal markings.

BIG BEN

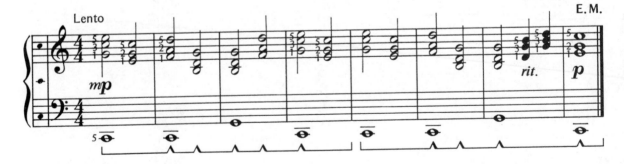

Chorale and *We Gather Together* are written in **hymn style**, in which the melody is harmonized with chords divided between the two hands.

Play these two hymns with indirect pedaling, aiming for a perfectly smooth connection between each tone or chord.

CHORALE

Robert Schumann (1810-1856)

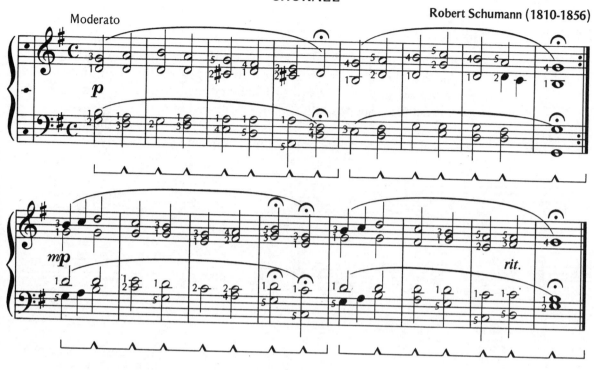

WE GATHER TOGETHER

Traditional

IMPROVISATION

Pentatonic Improvisation

Using the pentatonic scale, improvise a "bagpipe" sound by playing open fifths with the left hand in $\frac{6}{8}$ or $\frac{3}{4}$ meter, as below. The open fifth Gb—Db seems to blend most easily with black-key melodies in this style, and the accompaniment sounds fuller when it is played in the lower register.

An even more effective bagpipe sound will result with the addition of a grace-note figure to the open-fifth accompaniment, as below.

Now try improvising your own melodies over the open-fifth accompaniment. Look at some of the pieces in this book in $\frac{6}{8}$ or $\frac{3}{4}$ meter to give you ideas for various melody rhythms. The next piece, *Scotch Kilt*, will give you additional ideas.

SCOTCH KILT

Moderato   E.M.

For a "Western" sound, play one of the following ostinato accompaniment figures with the left hand.

In the pentatonic scale, two positions of this accompaniment are possible:

Here are two variations of the accompaniment in different meters:

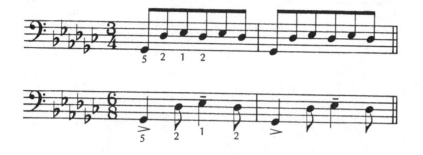

Next try improvising your own melodies over one of these Western accompaniments. Play *Lonesome Trail* to give yourself some ideas.

LONESOME TRAIL

12-Bar Blues Improvisation

Practice playing the 12-bar blues in various keys, using rhythms such as a dotted eighth note followed by a sixteenth note, with or without a triplet figure containing the blue note, as below. A **triplet** is a group of three notes which is played in the same time as two notes of the same value.

The triplet figure has a slur and a 3 either above or below it:

After playing *Step Along Blues*, try improvising melodies using the same dotted note combination along with triplet figures, such as

To get the right rhythm for the triplet figure, chant "*step*-a-long" as you play each triplet in the piece.

STEP ALONG BLUES

Try making up a blue-note improvisation in other keys. *Unfinished Blues* is in the key of F. Play the five measures given, and then improvise your own ending to it.

UNFINISHED BLUES

etc.

Now try playing a syncopated rhythm (page 131), similar to the rhythm in *Syncopated Blues*.

count: 1 + 2 + 3 + 4 +

SYNCOPATED BLUES

Next begin improvising melodies that extend the five-finger pattern. Let's begin with a scale as the melody. In *Scaling the Blues*, the major scales of C, F, and G are used.

SCALING THE BLUES

Now try playing the piece with a dotted rhythm for the scale melody, like this: ♩. ♪♪. ♪♪. ♪♪. ♪. Another possibility is to play the melody descending rather than ascending. All kinds of arrangements can be improvised by varying the extended melody-note combinations and using different rhythmic patterns. Here are just three examples:

You can improvise a boogie-woogie pattern by using the tones in the basic triad of the accompaniment (tones 1, 3, 5) plus the *sixth* tone, and the *seventh* tone lowered by one half step:

If you add the lowered seventh tone to the left-hand part as well, you will have a V^7 (dominant-seventh) accompaniment.

Play *Boogie-Woogie Blues*. Next try reversing the parts so that the left hand plays the boogie-woogie pattern while the right hand plays the chords. Finally, start improvising your own melodies with different rhythmic patterns, using the boogie-woogie pattern as a starting point.

BOOGIE-WOOGIE BLUES

To this point, your blues improvisations have been using the same harmony throughout the measure. Now let's begin using the alternating pattern of I—IV$^6_4$—I in each measure of the accompaniment. For example, in the key of F, the accompaniment will be as follows, with the IV chord in the second inversion, as you first encountered it (pages 64-65):

After practicing this accompaniment pattern, play the *I—IV—I Blues.* Then try transposing the piece to various keys of your choice. Now improvise your own melodies, using this accompaniment pattern.

I—IV—I BLUES

Next try using this same accompaniment pattern with changes of rhythm, such as a dotted eighth note followed by a sixteenth, as illustrated:

A "rocking bass" accompaniment is quite effective for jazz improvisation. The accompaniment uses the following ostinato pattern:

A grace-note figure is used to give a more "jazzy" sound.

ROCKING IN C

Transpose this piece to F. Using the rocking-bass accompaniment, improvise your own melodies. Feel free to move to various registers as you experiment with jazz and blues improvisations.

There are many kinds of ostinato accompaniment patterns that are quite effective for blues improvisation. *Over Easy Blues* uses an ostinato pattern with I, vi⁶, and a V⁷ chord borrowed from another key. When moving from the vi⁶ to the V⁷, repeat the two bottom tones in the left hand and move the thumb tone up a *half step*.

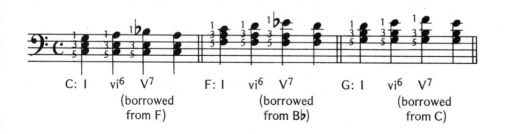

After practicing the accompaniment pattern, play *Over Easy Blues*. Then improvise your own melodies, using this accompaniment pattern and some of the suggested patterns on page 166.

OVER EASY BLUES

Ostinato accompaniment patterns

5.

An ostinato pattern with a minor ii chord is effective for improvising blues melodies. Note the interval of a diminished seventh (d7) in the second chord.

After practicing the accompaniment pattern, play *Step-Around Blues.* Then improvise your own melodies using this accompaniment pattern.

STEP-AROUND BLUES

Now try improvising melodies using the **blues scale**, which is made up of scale degrees 1, 4, 5, and 8, plus the *third*, *fifth*, and *seventh* tones, each lowered by one half step:

The blues scale

First work to get the "feel" of the blues scale. Then begin accenting the *second* and *fourth* beats as you play *Up-and-Down Blues.* Next try improvising your own melodies with different rhythmic patterns based on the blues scale.

UP-AND-DOWN BLUES

*The top tone of the seventh chord may be omitted throughout if necessary.

Now try improvising melodies based on the blues scale. *Conversational Blues* uses the ostinato accompaniment pattern I—I—I^7—IV$^6_4$—I in a question-and-answer dialogue. The "question" is stated in the left hand:

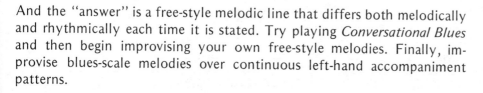

C: I   V^7 IV$^6_4$ F: I   V^7 IV$^6_4$ G: I   V^7 IV$^6_4$
(borrowed)   (borrowed)   (borrowed)

And the "answer" is a free-style melodic line that differs both melodically and rhythmically each time it is stated. Try playing *Conversational Blues* and then begin improvising your own free-style melodies. Finally, improvise blues-scale melodies over continuous left-hand accompaniment patterns.

CONVERSATIONAL BLUES

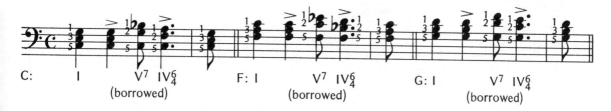

CREATIVE MUSIC AND HARMONIZATION

1. The two phrases below extend beyond the five-finger position. Improvise matching phrases for each, using an extended range. Write the phrases on the staffs provided. Then add fingerings to the phrases and circle those that are extended (contraction, extension, and so on).

a.

b.

2. Next improvise matching phrases in extended range for each of the following phrases and harmonize with I, IV$_4^6$, and V$_5^6$ chords. Write the phrases, chords, and the chord numbers on the staffs provided.

a.

I IV$_4^6$

b.

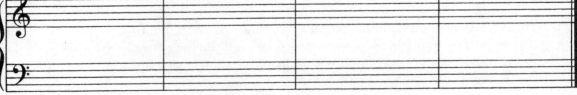

I IV$_4^6$ I V$_5^6$

3. Add the indicated accompaniment pattern to the melodies below. Play the first melody with the waltz pattern (a), then with the arpeggio pattern (b).

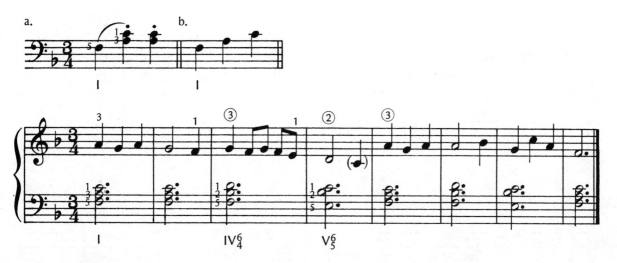

Play the second melody with the Alberti bass pattern (a), then with the extended-arpeggio pattern (b).

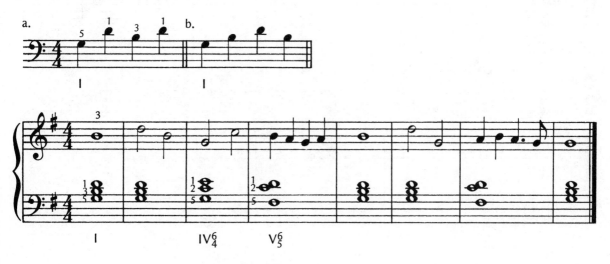

Play the last melody with a broken-chord pattern:

4. Harmonize the following melodies with I, IV$^6_4$, and V$^6_5$ chords in the same accompaniment style as in the first measure of each. Add chord numbers below each as indicated.

a.

b.

5. Using triads on the white keys as the left-hand accompaniment, improvise melodies that will blend with the accompaniment. Use the following as an example.

Now try changing the arrangement of triads in the accompaniment.
Here are several suggestions:

*The fingering $\frac{1}{2}$ may be substituted here for $\frac{1}{3}$.
 45

Write your own example consisting of two four-measure phrases using one
of these accompaniments or one of your own choice in a similar style.

6. Improvise melodies to the chords below in as many different keys as possible:

a. $\frac{3}{4}$ I | IV$^6_4$ | I | V$^6_5$ | I | IV$^6_4$ | V$^6_5$ | I ‖

b. $\frac{4}{4}$ I ii | I IV$^6_4$ | V$^6_5$ V$^6_5$ | I | I ii | I IV$^6_4$ | I V$^6_5$ | I ‖

7. Improvise a melody to the following accompaniment:

8. Write a matching phrase for each of the following melodies with the same style of accompaniment used for the first phrase.

a. Open fifths

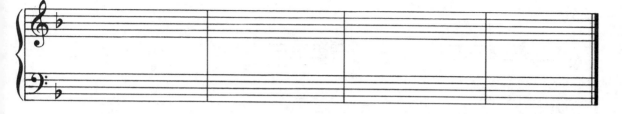

b. Walking-bass ostinato pattern

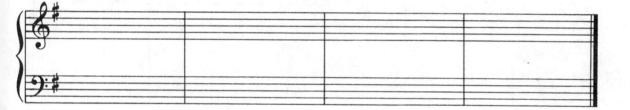

c. Western ostinato

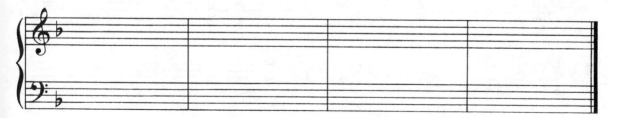

d. Hymn style

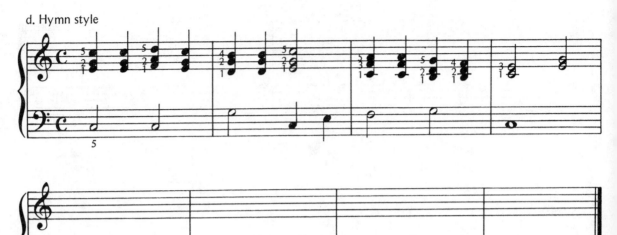

e. Triad figures/Fifths in accompaniment

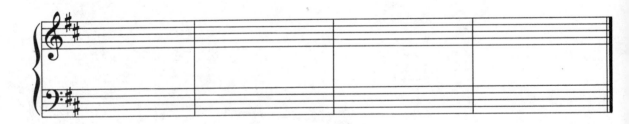

f. Parallel sixths/Fourths in accompaniment

9. A melodic skeleton and one way of completing it are given below. Use it as an example in completing melodic skeleton 2.

Melodic skeleton 1

Melodic skeleton 1 completed

Now improvise your own completion to melodic skeleton 1.

Melodic skeleton 2

Improvise some completions for melodic skeleton 2 and write down your favorite one.

Melodic skeleton 2 completed

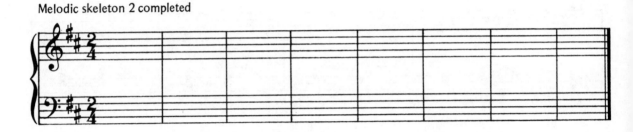

10. The A section of a composition in two-part song form (AB) is given below. It consists of four phrases, two for A and two for A'. Write a B section consisting of four more phrases (B and B') on the staves on the next page. Contrast the melodic content but keep the same accompaniment style and remain in the same key.

A′   phrase 3

phrase 4

B

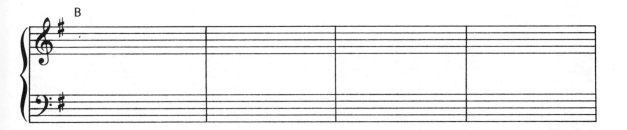

B′

180

11. Write your own composition in two-part song form (AB) or three-part song form (ABA). Select a key, meter signature, accompaniment style, tempo, expression and dynamic markings, and pedal markings (if pedal is desired). Indicate any fingering changes. First notate the music in pencil and make any necessary corrections. Then write the final version on the staves provided.

SIGHTREADING STUDIES

The first step is to determine the key of the study. Next observe the meter signature. Quickly scan the example to look at rhythmic and melodic patterns and any harmonic patterns. Note changes of fingering where they occur. Try to observe all dynamic and expression markings. Finally, be sure to look ahead as you play—and don't look at the keys!

Melodies in Parallel Motion

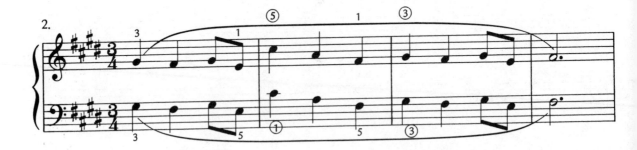

3.

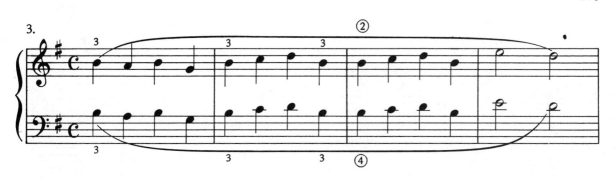

4.

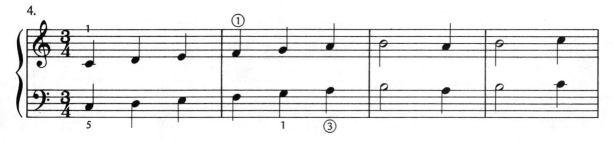

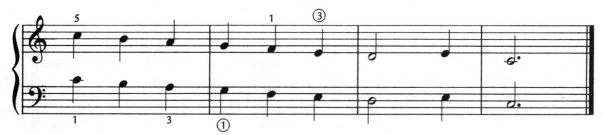

5.

Accompanied Melodies

1.

2.

3.

7.

8.

9.

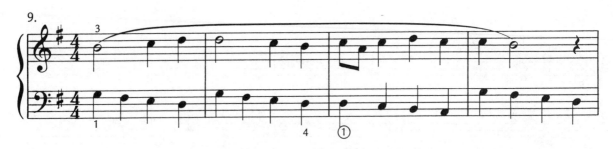

10.

Pedal Studies

1.

2.

ENSEMBLE PIECES

Four Hands, One Piano

WHAT CHILD IS THIS? (Greensleeves)

Moderato

English (arr. E. M.)

VALSE DU CHOCOLAT AUX AMANDES
(Chocolate-with-Almonds Waltz)

Erik Satie (1866–1925) (arr. E.M.)

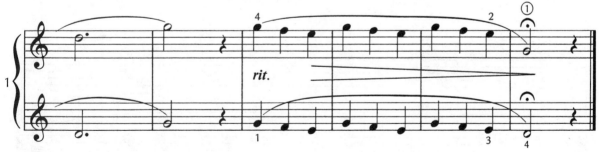

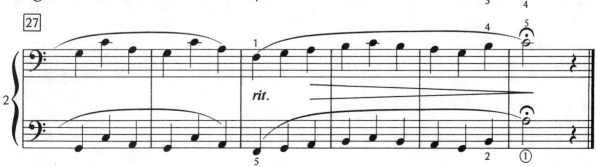

STREETS OF LAREDO

Moderato

American cowboy tune (arr. E. M.)

SHE'LL BE COMIN' ROUND THE MOUNTAIN

Southern mountain song (arr. E. M.)

LIEBESTRAUME THEME

Franz Liszt (1811–1886) (arr. E. M.)

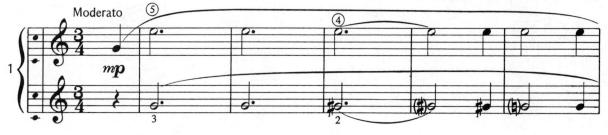

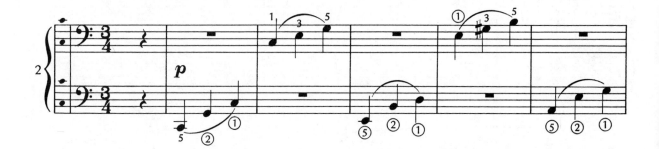

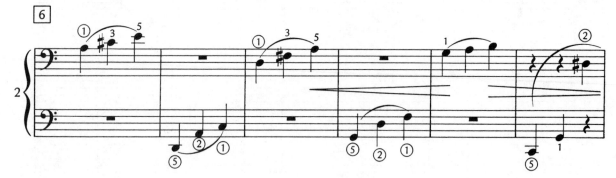

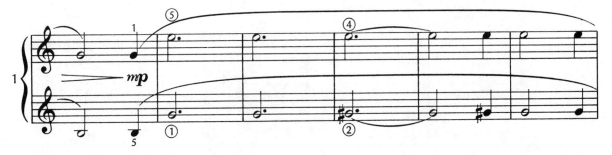

 12

18

Four Hands, Two Pianos

OLD MACDONALD HAD A FARM*

American (arr. E. M.)

*This piece may be played four hands at one piano if the Piano 1 part is played one octave higher than written.

GAÎTÉ PARISIENNE

Allegro

Jacques Offenbach

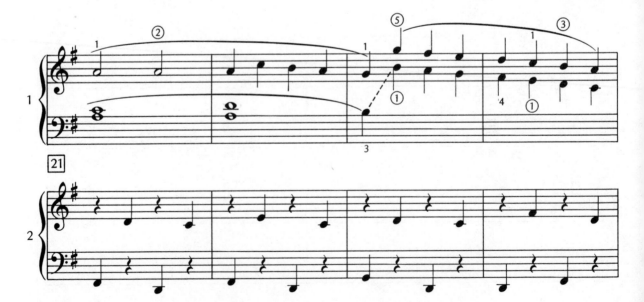

25

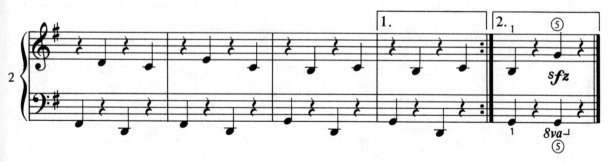

29

AU CLAIR DE LA LUNE

French (arr. E.M.)

*Optional

REVIEW OF TERMS AND SYMBOLS

Make sure you understand the following terms and symbols, which were introduced in this unit. Check the index to find the discussion of any term you need to review.

Keyboard and Notation

kinds of fingering
   extension
   substitution
   contraction
   crossing
first and second endings
damper pedal
direct pedaling
una corda (soft pedal)
indirect pedaling

Performance

alla breve (¢ or $\frac{2}{2}$)
con moto
grazioso
sempre staccato

Theory

major scale
scale degrees
primary chords
secondary chords
interval
   perfect
   major
   minor
   diminished
   augmented
inverted triad
inverted dominant-seventh chord
modulation
dissonance
triplet
syncopation

Style and Structure

round
binary form (AB)
ternary form (ABA)
accompaniment patterns
   waltz
   arpeggio
   Alberti bass
   ostinato
   walking bass
bitonality
hymn style
blues scale

4

TONALITY AND ATONALITY

This unit introduces minor scales, scales of other modes, the chromatic scale, and the whole-tone scale, together with pieces based on these scales. Bitonality, atonality—including twelve-tone technique—and additional innovative notations are also introduced.

MINOR SCALES

Each minor scale is built from a corresponding major scale with the same key signature; this major scale is referred to as the **relative major**. For example, the F major scale is the relative major of the D minor scale (and the D minor scale is the **relative minor** of the F major scale) because both scales have one flat in their key signature:

The **natural minor scale** is formed by beginning on the sixth tone of its relative major and continuing up for an octave:

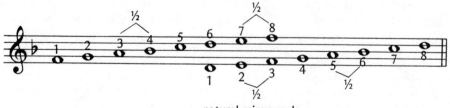

natural minor scale

Note that while the half steps occur between tones 3 and 4 and between tones 7 and 8 in the major scale, they occur between tones 2 and 3 and between tones 5 and 6 in the natural minor scale.

Besides the natural form, there are two other forms of the minor scale—the harmonic and the melodic. The **harmonic minor scale** is probably the most frequently used form of the three. It is the same as the natural minor scale with the exception of the seventh tone, which is raised one half step with the use of an accidental:

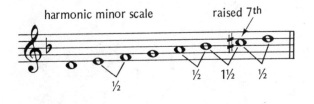

Note that the half steps in the harmonic minor scale occur between tones 2 and 3, between tones 5 and 6, and between tones 7 and 8. The raised seventh tone creates an interval of a step and a half (three half steps) between tones 6 and 7.*

The **melodic minor scale** is the same as the natural minor scale, except that the sixth and seventh tones are raised one half step in its ascending form. The descending melodic minor scale is identical to the natural minor form:

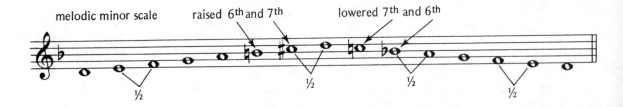

Note that the half steps in the melodic minor scale occur between tones 2 and 3 and between tones 7 and 8 ascending, and between tones 2 and 3 and tones 5 and 6 descending.

MINOR KEY SIGNATURES

Since each minor scale and its relative major scale have the same key signature, the key of a piece cannot be determined by looking only at the key signature. Look at the final tone of the piece (particularly the lowest tone of the final chord), which will invariably be the key tone, or tonic. In addition, look for tones 1, 3, and 5 of the tonic triad at the beginning and at the end of the piece. Your ear can also be of great help in determining whether the piece has a major or a minor sound to it.

*Note that by raising the third and sixth tones of the harmonic minor scale, you will be playing what is called the parallel major scale, as both scales begin with the same tonic tone. (The reverse is also true. By lowering the third and sixth tones of a major scale, you will be playing the parallel harmonic minor scale.) There is no other relationship between parallel scales. Unlike relative scales, parallel scales do not share the same key signature.

If you know the major key signatures, but are not completely certain of the minor key signatures, remember this: the minor key is *three half steps down* from its relative major key. For example, if the key signature has two sharps, the piece is either in D major or, counting down three half steps, B minor:

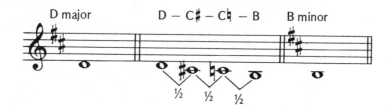

Here is a list of all major-minor key signature pairs:

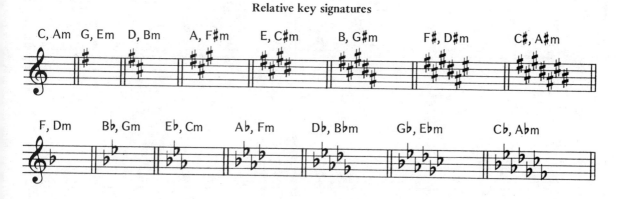

The following chart illustrates each minor scale in harmonic form (from which the other two forms can be worked out). Practice playing the scales, first with hands separately, then with hands together. Be sure to observe the fingerings provided.

Harmonic minor scales and fingerings

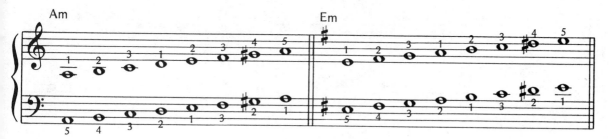

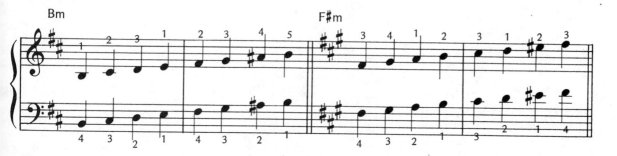

206

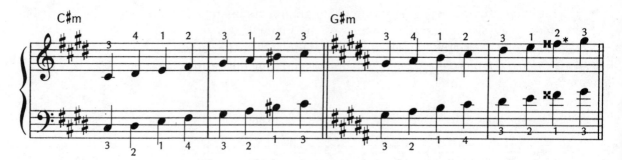

*A double sharp (✖) raises a tone two half steps or one whole step.

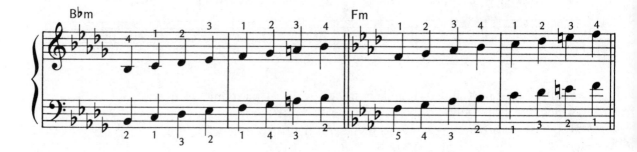

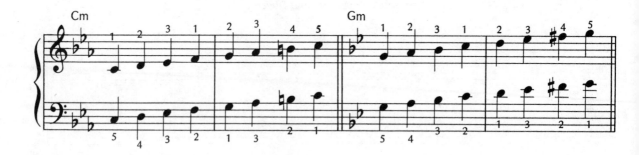

Practice playing the chord progression i—iv$_4^6$—i—V$_5^6$—i with the left hand in all minor keys, as shown below. Use the fifth tone of the five-finger pattern as the first tone (tonic) of each subsequent chord progression. Remember not to look at the keys. Try to develop a feel for the progression and anticipate the changing of chords.

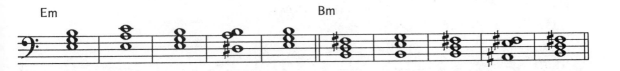

Another way of practicing the i–iv$^6_4$–i–V$^6_5$–i chord progression is to play the chords with the right hand while playing the root (or letter name) of each chord with the left hand, as shown below:

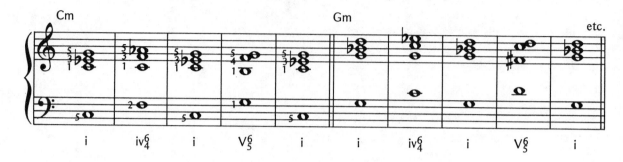

Hatikvah, the Israeli national anthem, uses the natural form of the D minor scale.

HATIKVAH

Volga Boatmen and *Joshua Fought the Battle of Jericho* use the
natural form of the C minor scale and the harmonic form of the D minor
scale, respectively.

VOLGA BOATMEN

JOSHUA FOUGHT THE BATTLE OF JERICHO

OTHER MODES

The word **mode** means the same as the word *way;* that is, a particular mode is a particular way of arranging whole steps and half steps in scale form. For roughly the last three hundred years, most Western music has used the major and minor modes or scales. But there are other modes, some of which are used in our folk tunes and in the music of other cultures. Each mode has its own arrangement of whole steps and half steps, and each can be constructed on the white keys alone, as illustrated below. (When the scales of these modes are transposed, accidentals must of course be added to preserve the half-step arrangement.)

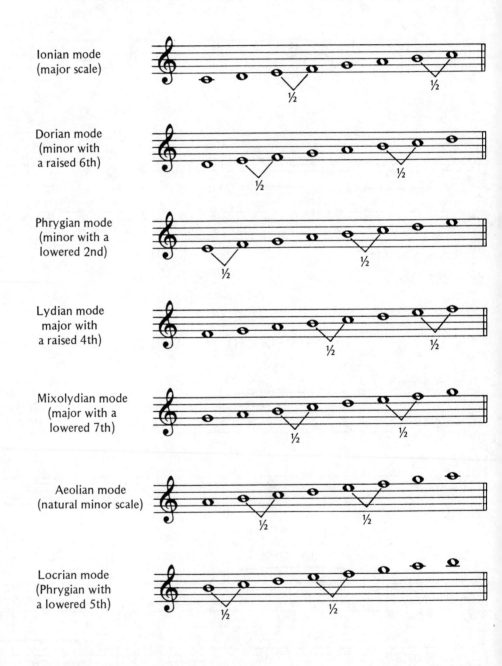

Both *Aeolian Lullaby* and *Sakura,* a Japanese tune, use the Aeolian mode (the natural minor scale).

AEOLIAN LULLABY

Joan Hansen

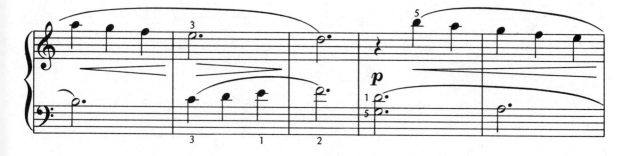

From *Music of Our Time*, Book I. Reprinted by permission of Waterloo Music Company Limited.

SAKURA

From *Music of Our Time*, Book I. Reprinted by permission of Waterloo Music Company Limited.

Scarborough Fair uses the Dorian mode, beginning on E:

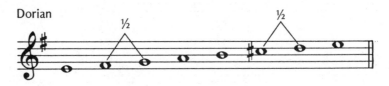

SCARBOROUGH FAIR

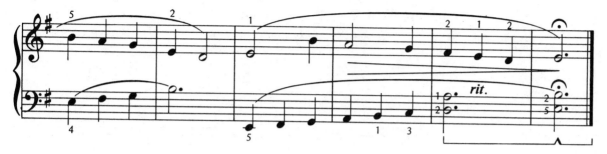

Old Joe Clark is in the Mixolydian mode, which sounds like the major scale with a lowered seventh degree. This mode is frequently used in the jazz idiom.

OLD JOE CLARK

214

Spanish Folk Melody uses the Phrygian mode, which sounds like the natural minor scale with a lowered second degree. The Phrygian mode is frequently used in Spanish flamenco music.

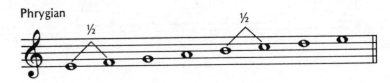

SPANISH FOLK MELODY

Sharp Four is in the Lydian mode, which sounds like the major scale with a raised fourth degree.

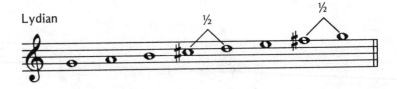

SHARP FOUR

Arthur Frackenpohl (born 1924)

Marche Slav uses the Byzantine scale (also called the Hungarian minor scale), which is the harmonic minor scale with a raised fourth degree. Many Russian composers often use this scale.

MARCHE SLAV

Peter Ilich Tchaikovsky (1840-1893)

THE CHROMATIC SCALE

The **chromatic scale** is constructed by using half steps only; it contains all twelve tones. Notice the fingering for this scale as given below. The third finger is always used on the black keys, and the thumb is used on most of the white keys. But the *second* finger is always used for the notes F and C in the right hand and for the notes E and B in the left hand.

Practice the chromatic scale ascending and descending, first with each hand separately, then with hands together. Be sure to observe the correct fingering:

chromatic scale ascending

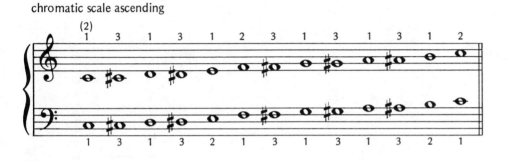

chromatic scale descending

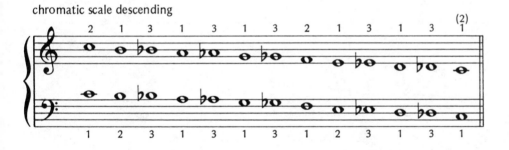

218

The following piece uses chromaticism in the melody and throughout the accompaniment.

CHROMATIC SKETCH

E. M.

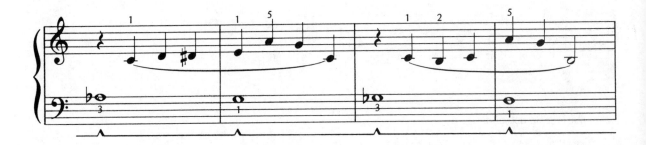

Chromatic Blues uses chromaticism throughout in the melody.

CHROMATIC BLUES

Easygoing   E. M.

PANDIATONICISM

Pandiatonicism arose early in the twentieth century as a reaction against the chromaticism of such composers as Wagner, Ravel, and Debussy. Most of the tones are taken from one scale, frequently major and often C major, with no or very few accidentals, as illustrated by *Andantino.* Thus the term "white-note writing," as pandiatonicism is often called.

Another twentieth-century practice illustrated by this piece is the irregular phrase lengths used to accommodate the rhythmic patterns.

ANDANTINO
(from *Les Cinq Doigts*)

Igor Stravinsky (1882-1971)

Fine

Da Capo al Fine

Used by kind permission of J. & W. Chester/Edition Wilhelm Hansen London Limited.

THE WHOLE-TONE SCALE

The **whole-tone scale** is constructed by using whole steps only; it contains
six tones:

Some early twentieth-century music, notably that of Claude Debussy
(1862-1918), incorporates the use of the whole-tone scale.

Veiled, atmospheric effects can be produced by using the damper
pedal to sustain whole-tone groupings, as in Stan Applebaum's *Prelude in
Miniature*. Play this whole-tone piece with a very light touch.

PRELUDE IN MINIATURE

■ ♪ = 144 is a **metronome marking.** A metronome is a time-keeping
instrument, in which either a pendulum or electricity produces a
ticking sound at any desired speed. This particular marking means to
set the metronome at 144, with the resultant ticking sound equivalent
to the duration of an eighth-note beat, 144 beats a minute.

For fun, try rewriting a familiar tune, using the whole-tone scale. It will sound somewhat changed! Here is an example:

NAME THAT TUNE

E. M.

Take other familiar tunes and arrange them in whole-tone settings by altering tones to fit the whole-step pattern. Then try improvising melodies that use the whole-tone scale.

BITONALITY

As mentioned in Unit 3, a **bitonal** piece is one in which two keys are used simulatneously. *Pomp* is an example. The right hand is in A, and the left hand in C.

Identify and practice the various triads with each hand and then both hands together before playing this piece.

POMP

Vincent Persichetti

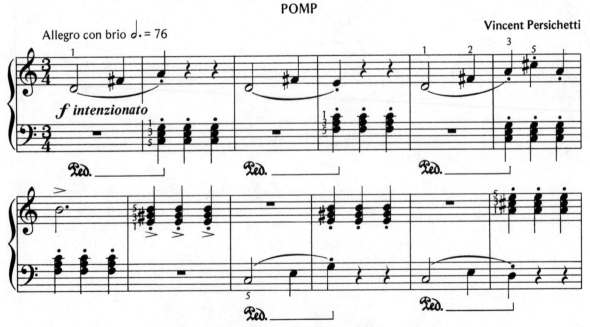

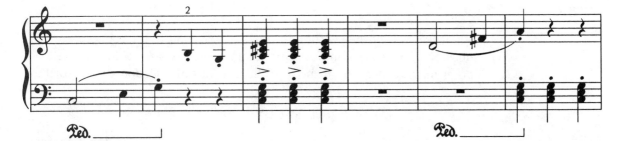

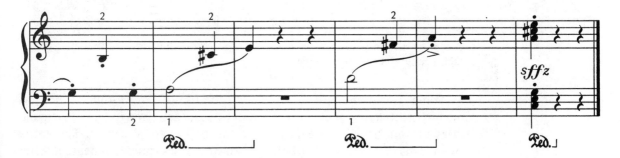

ATONALITY

An **atonal** piece is one without a tonal center—that is, it has no key, and no one tone seems more important than any other. In *Atonal Study*, the composer makes much use of the melodic intervals of a second and a fourth.

ATONAL STUDY

Stan Applebaum

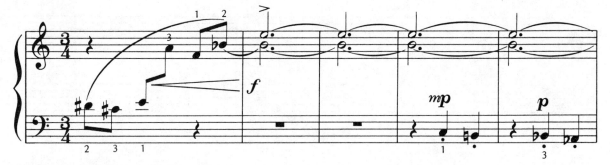

Some atonal music is written with the use of **twelve-tone technique,** in which all twelve tones of the chromatic scale are arranged in a particular **series** or **tone row.** These tones have no key or tonal center. The entire row is usually heard in full before it or any of its tones is repeated. After the row has been introduced, it may be varied in a number of ways: it may be used in **inversion** (upside down); in **retrograde** (backward); and in **retrograde inversion** (upside down and backward).

In *Twelve-Tone Study*, the series of twelve tones is introduced in the first two measures in both hands; it is then repeated four times in various rhythmic patterns. Does the composer use any of the variations mentioned above?

TWELVE-TONE STUDY

Stan Applebaum

The tone row in *Row, Row, Row Your Tone* sounds nothing like the familiar tune to which the title alludes. The row is stated and then repeated without any variation.

Try writing a new melody to familiar words, using a tone row of your own.

A tone row or series

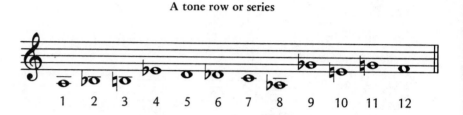

1　2　3　4　5　6　7　8　9　10　11　12

ROW, ROW, ROW YOUR TONE

Noona

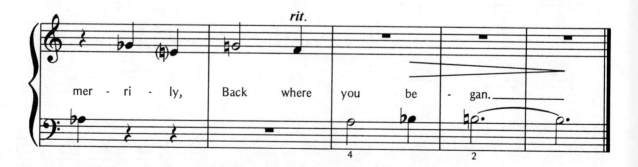

An innovative notation is any notation invented by a composer to indicate special effects and how they should be performed.

In *5-White-Note Clusters* the white stemmed rectangles are half-note clusters (see page 26), and in *Seashore* they are dotted-half-note clusters. The number 5 that appears above them specifies the number of tones in each, and the position of the rectangle on the staff specifies the exact pitches. For example, in the first measure of *5-White-Note Clusters*, the pitches are C to G in the first rectangle, and A to E in the second one.

Play the clusters in these two pieces with your fingers or your fist. As mentioned earlier, clusters can also be played with the knuckles, the palm of the open hand, or the arm. Sometimes clusters are even played with pieces of wood or other devices.

5-WHITE-NOTE CLUSTERS

Ross Lee Finney (born 1906)

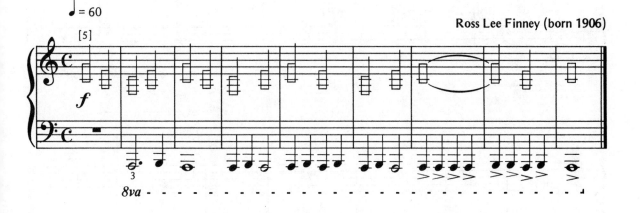

From *32 Piano Games*. Copyright © 1960 by Henmar Press Inc. (C. F. Peters Corporation). Reprinted by permission of the publisher. All rights reserved.

SEASHORE

Ross Lee Finney

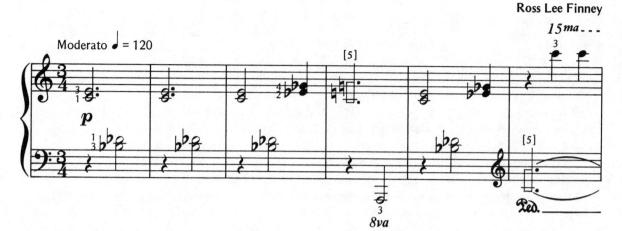

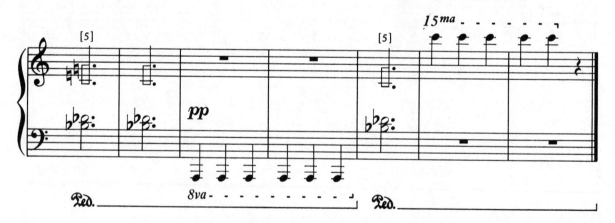

- **15ma** means to play 15 notes (two octaves) higher than written.

In *Winter,* the composer has used several innovative notations, in addition to clusters:

$\bigvee$ or $\bigwedge$ pause for an indeterminate length of time make a ritardando as indicated by the increasingly wide distance between the notes.

Finney has also omitted meter signature and bar lines, to give the performer the freedom to interpret the music in his or her own way.

WINTER

- The parallel lines between the clusters indicate a **tremolo**, which is a quick alternation from one cluster to the other.

BITONAL IMPROVISATION

First play the examples provided below. Then, using the left-hand patterns given, improvise your own melodies. Finally, try creating new left-hand patterns to accompany your own melodies. Think of changing meters, using different registers, and trying out various tempo changes as well as experimenting with new dynamic shadings.

1. Improvise a bitonal melody with the right hand to the left-hand accompaniment of open fifths, which is in the key of C. The right-hand melody begun below is in E.

2. Using a black-key ostinato pattern as the left-hand accompaniment, improvise white-key melodies with the right hand.

3. Using black-key open fifths in the left hand, improvise white-key melodies and harmonic intervals with the right hand. Use the "toccata" style below to start with.

4. Using a left-hand pattern based on the whole-tone scale, improvise melodies that will blend with the accompaniment. Use the pattern below as a model.

5. Improvise melodies to a chromatic left-hand accompaniment, such as the one begun below.

SIGHTREADING STUDIES

As you sightread these studies, *do not slow down* to find the notes or correct mistakes. If you encounter difficulties, isolate the passage later and work out the problem with careful study and practice.

1. Aeolian

2. Phrygian

3. Dorian

4. Lydian

5. Mixolydian

6. Byzantine (Hungarian minor)

234

ENSEMBLE PIECES

Four Hands, Two Pianos

FOR THE KID NEXT DOOR

Soulima Stravinsky (born 1910)

12

18

24

GOOD NIGHT

Mikhail Ziv (born 1921)

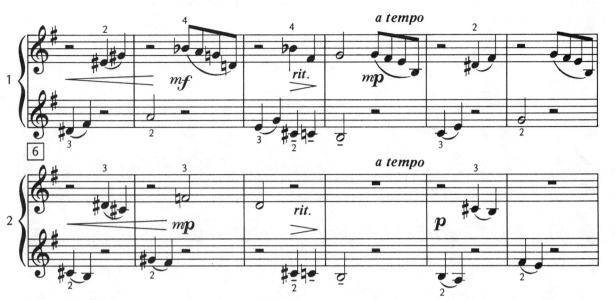

Eight Hands, Four Pianos

PRAYER TIME

Like an organ ♩ = 44

Norman dello Joio (born 1913)

(Bells)

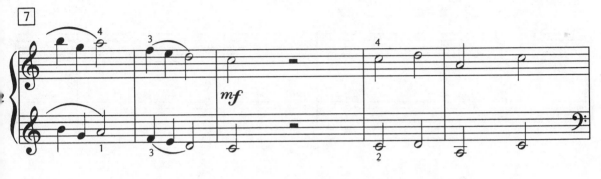

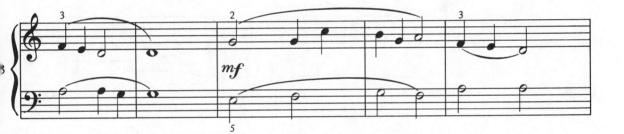

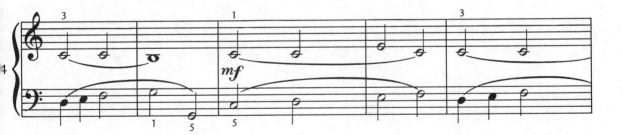

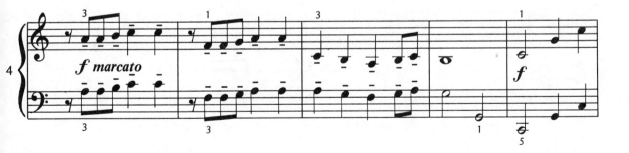

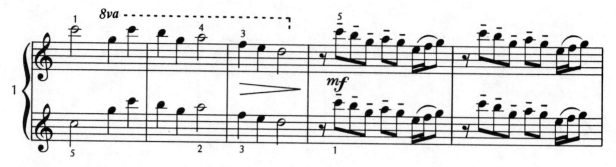

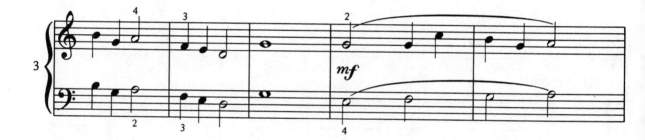

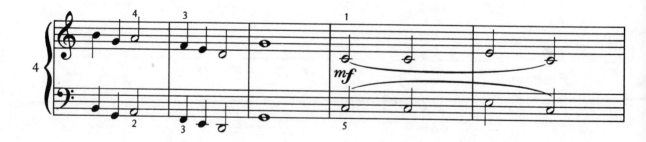

27

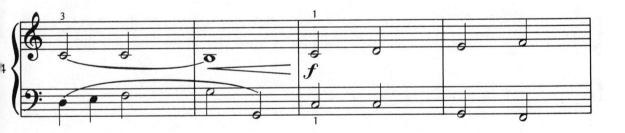

31

REVIEW OF TERMS AND SYMBOLS

Make sure you understand the following terms and symbols which were introduced in this unit. Check the index to find the discussion of any term you need to review.

Keyboard and Notation

metronome marking

Performance

con forza
15ma
tremolo

Theory

relative minor

relative major
minor scale
  natural
  harmonic
  melodic
modes
  Ionian
  Aeolian
  Dorian
  Phrygian
  Lydian
  Mixolydian
  Locrian

Byzantine scale
chromatic scale
whole-tone scale

Style and Structure

pandiatonicism
atonality
tone row
  inversion
  retrograde
  retrograde inversion
twelve-tone technique

5

LETTER-NAME CHORD SYMBOLS

Many printed versions of folk tunes and popular songs do not include any accompaniment, but identify the chords merely by letter names. Letter names are used instead of roman numerals because they are much simpler and faster to read. Both in printed songs and in this unit, the letter-name chord symbols are meant to be a guide for your use in improvising your own accompaniments.

Note: As you'll see below, letter-name chord symbols indicate root position only of the given chord, not inversions. Depending on the accompaniment pattern you choose, you have the option of using any chord in its root position or in one of the inversions studied earlier—particularly the second inversion of IV (IV$_4^6$) and the first inversion of V^7 (V$_5^6$).

LETTER NAMES OF I, IV, AND V^7 CHORDS

Remember that the I, IV, and V^7 chords are named for their position in the scale:

> I chords are constructed on the *first* degree of the scale
> IV chords are constructed on the *fourth* degree of the scale
> V^7 chords are constructed on the *fifth* degree of the scale

So in the key of C, for example, the letter names of these three chords are C, F, and G^7:

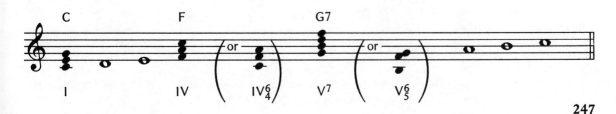

The following chart gives the letter names of the I, IV, and V^7 chords in all major keys:

Key	I	IV	V^7
C	C	F	G^7
G	G	C	D^7
D	D	G	A^7
A	A	D	E^7
E	E	A	B^7
B	B	E	$F\sharp^7$
F♯)	F♯)	B)	C♯^{7})
G♭)	G♭)	C♭)	D♭^{7})
C♯)	C♯)	F♯)	G♯^{7})
D♭)	D♭)	G♭)	A♭^{7})
A♭	A♭	D♭	E♭^{7}
E♭	E♭	A♭	B♭^{7}
B♭	B♭	E♭	F^7
F	F	B♭	C^7

MELODIES WITH LETTER-NAME CHORD SYMBOLS

Letter names rather than roman numerals have been used for the I, IV, and V^7 chords in the following melodies. Refer back to the section in Unit 3 called Broken-Chord Accompaniment Patterns as a guide in your choice of appropriate patterns, and improvise an accompaniment for some of these melodies, using the indicated harmonies.

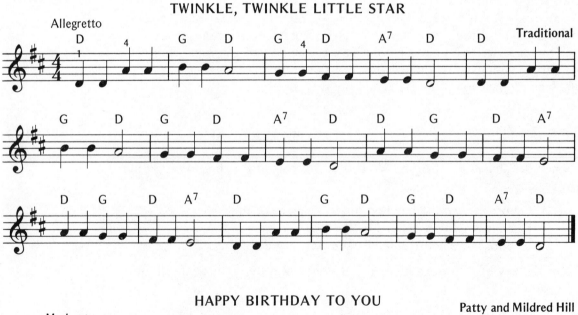

TWINKLE, TWINKLE LITTLE STAR

HAPPY BIRTHDAY TO YOU

AMERICA

Henry Carey

AMERICA THE BEAUTIFUL

Samuel Ward

CAMPTOWN RACES

Stephen Foster

De Camp-town la - dies sing dis song, Doo - dah, Doo - dah. De

Camp - town race - track five mile long, Oh! doo - dah day.

Gwine to run all night, Gwine to run all day, I'll____

bet my mon-ey on de bob - tail nag, Some - bod - y bet on de bay.

RED RIVER VALLEY

Please come sit by my side ere you leave me,_____ Do not has-ten to bid me a-dieu;_____ Just re-mem-ber the Red Ri-ver Val-ley,_____ And the sweet-heart who loves you so true._____

HOME ON THE RANGE

Oh give me a home where the buf-fa-lo roam, Where the deer and the an-te-lope play,_____ Where sel-dom is heard a dis-cour-ag-ing word, And the skies are not cloud-y all day._____ Home, home on the range,_____ Where the deer and the an-te-lope play.___Where sel-dom is heard a dis-cour-ag-ing word, And the skies are not cloud-y all day.___

ARKANSAS TRAVELER

ALOHA OE

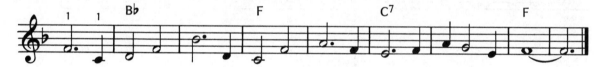

GOODBYE OL' PAINT

In addition to I, IV, and V^7, the following melodies include the secondary chords of ii, iii, and vi. Follow the same procedure in improvising accompaniments for these melodies, using the indicated harmonies.

BILL BAILEY, WON'T YOU PLEASE COME HOME?

Allegretto

Hughie Cannon

WALTZING MATILDA

Moderato

Australian

MICHAEL, ROW THE BOAT ASHORE

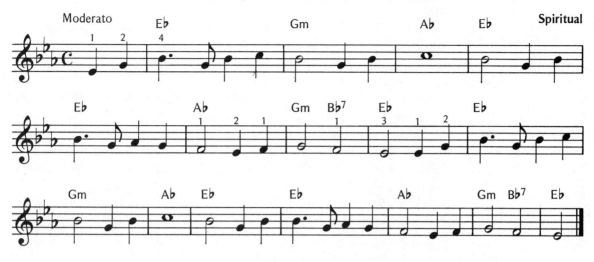

AMAZING GRACE

MOLLY MALONE

STRUMMING ACCOMPANIMENTS

Strumming is a kind of accompaniment that uses both hands, while the melody is usually provided by another individual or group, vocal or instrumental. This type of accompaniment is very effective for community sing programs.

In strumming, it is important to remember that the *left* hand plays individual tones of the chord. For example, with a C chord the left hand would play the root tone C most frequently and would perhaps alternate the C with G, the fifth of the chord. If extended use were made of the C chord as a harmony, the left hand would probably play E, the third tone, as well.

The *right* hand plays a block chord, either in root position on in first or second inversion. Remember that the left hand and the right hand always alternate in a strummed accompaniment. Play and hum the following two examples of songs with strummed accompaniments.

DIXIE

SWEET BETSY FROM PIKE

An easy way to practice strumming is to play the root of the chord with the left thumb, and then to play the fifth transposed down one octave with the fourth finger, as illustrated below. Practice playing this pattern in all keys.

Next, with the right hand, play basic triads in root position in major through all the keys. Then do the same in minor. The right hand alternates with the left, which remains unchanged.

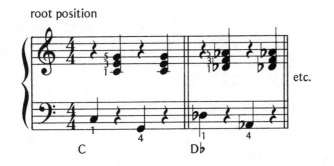

Finally, with the right hand, practice these same triads in first inversion and then in second inversion through all the major and minor keys, as illustrated below:

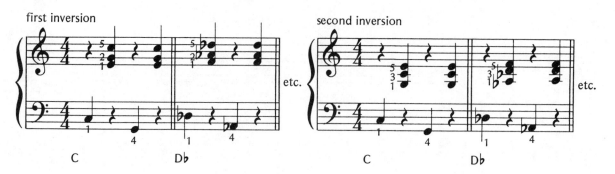

first inversion   second inversion

Sing or hum some of the melodies presented earlier in this unit and accompany yourself with this strumming technique. Then experiment with a few of your own strumming accompaniments. Try using the third of the chord in the left hand and try alternating root-position chords and inverted chords in the right hand.

ARPEGGIO ACCOMPANIMENTS

Diminished and Augmented Intervals

Besides major and minor triads, diminished and augmented triads are often used in the accompaniments of popular songs. In the table below, note the way diminished and augmented triads are formed:

triad	C major	C minor	C diminished	C augmented
symbol	C	Cm	C° (or C dim.)	C⁺ (or C aug.)
formation		lower the third tone one half step	lower the third and fifth tones one half step (when starting from a major triad)	raise the fifth tone one half step

First, in all keys, practice these four kinds of triads with the left hand as block chords in two octaves until you are familiar with the difference in their sound:

C   Cm   C°   C⁺

Next play the triads as arpeggios in two octaves with the left hand:

C   Cm   C°   C⁺

Finally, play the arpeggios as before, but omit the third tone from the first part of the arpeggio:

Practice playing this pattern not only ascending but descending as well. Be sure to observe the correct fingering, *and look away from the keys as much as possible!*

Improvise an arpeggio accompaniment for *Someone* to see how this kind of accompaniment can be used. Play the song first with hands separately, then with hands together. In measure 11 play the arpeggio pattern like this:

SOMEONE

Major and Minor Seventh Chords

Besides the dominant-seventh chord, the major and minor seventh chords are used frequently in the accompaniments of popular song melodies. All three of these chords are constructed similarly—they all have a third, fifth, and seventh tone above the root. It is the seventh that distinguishes the dominant-seventh chord from the major seventh chord, and the lowered third that distinguishes the minor seventh chord from the dominant-seventh chord:

chord	dominant-seventh	major seventh	minor seventh
symbol	G⁷	GM⁷	Gm⁷
formation	start with a major triad (root, third, fifth); add the eighth, forming an octave with the root; lower the eighth *one whole step*	start with a major triad (root, third, fifth); add the eighth, forming an octave with the root; lower the eighth *one half step*	start with a minor triad (root, third, fifth); add the eighth, forming an octave with the root; lower the eighth *one whole step*

The dominant-seventh and minor seventh chords lower the octave *one whole step*. The major seventh chord lowers the octave *one half step*. This is the easiest way to remember the difference between the chords.

As previously discussed, G⁷ uses tones from the key of C major. It is constructed on the fifth (or *dominant*) tone of that key, and that is why it is called a dominant-seventh chord.

GM⁷ uses tones from the key of G major. It uses the first, third, fifth, and seventh tones of the G major scale, and that is why it is called a major seventh chord.

Gm⁷ uses tones from the key of G minor. It uses the first, third, fifth, and seventh tones of the G minor scale, and that is why it is called a minor seventh chord.

Practice playing dominant-seventh, major seventh, and minor seventh chords in various keys, as illustrated below:

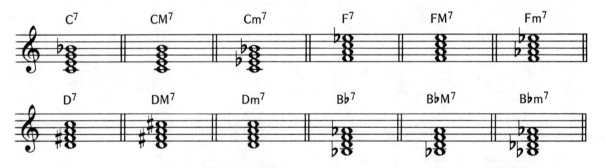

Next practice the three seventh chords in an arpeggio pattern, as illustrated below. Play this pattern in various keys, ascending and descending. Be sure to observe the correct fingering:

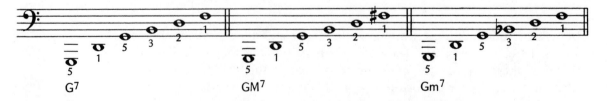

Using the arpeggio pattern, improvise an accompaniment for *This Love of Ours,* changing the harmonies as indicated by the letter-name chord

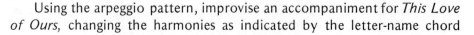

symbols. Be sure to include both the indicated harmonies in measures 3, 7, and 16. In these measures, play the arpeggio pattern like this:

THIS LOVE OF OURS

MORE
(Theme from *Mondo Cane*)

R. Ortolani and N. Oliviero

SOMEWHERE OVER THE RAINBOW

Harold Arlen

SOMEWHERE MY LOVE
(Lara's Theme from *Doctor Zhivago*)

Maurice Jarre

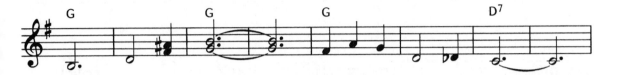

LETTER-NAME CHORD CHART

The following chart lists every chord discussed in this unit in all major and
minor keys. It is for your convenience in quickly forming the chords you
will need when you improvise accompaniments.

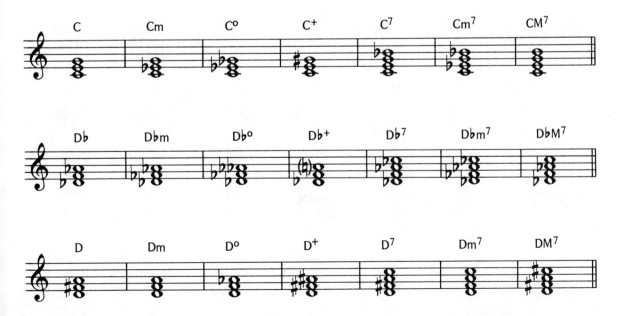

ENSEMBLE PIECES

FIDDLER ON THE ROOF

Jerry Bock (arr. E. M.)

EDELWEISS
(from *The Sound of Music*)

Richard Rodgers (arr. E. M.)

Slowly

6

TWENTY-FIVE PIANO CLASSICS

This unit consists of 25 solo keyboard pieces from the Baroque, Classical, Romantic, and contemporary periods, which vary in difficulty, style, length, and form. The pieces have been arranged by period rather than degree of difficulty.

In *Carnival*, the left hand uses an **ostinato** accompaniment throughout.

CARNIVAL

François Couperin (1668–1733)

The **dance suite** was an important instrumental form of the Baroque period (roughly 1600–1750). It consisted of a series of short dances or movements that were usually in AB (binary) form. A suite opened with an optional prelude, followed by an allemande, a courante, a sarabande, then one or more optional dances—such as a minuet, a bourrée, or a gavotte—and ended with a gigue.

The **minuet** is a graceful seventeenth-century French dance in $\frac{3}{4}$ time with a moderate tempo. Its name derives from the French word *menu* ("small"), in reference, perhaps, to the small steps taken by the dancers.

MINUET IN A MINOR

Andante

Henry Purcell (c. 1658–1695)

The **gavotte** is a French dance in $\frac{4}{4}$ time, with a moderate tempo. It usually starts on the third beat of the measure.

GAVOTTE

Moderato

Johann Georg Witthauer (1750–1802)

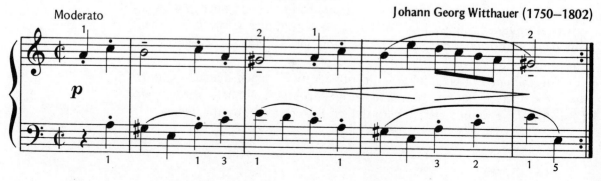

The **bourrée** is a French dance in $\frac{4}{4}$ time, starting with an upbeat. It is lively and spirited, and moves at a rather quick tempo.

BOURRÉE

Leopold Mozart

The **allemande** is a German dance (*allemande* in French means "German") in $\frac{4}{4}$ time with a moderate tempo. An allemande is frequently the first movement in a dance suite.

ALLEMANDE

The **sarabande** is a slow, stately Spanish dance in triple time, frequently played with an accent on the second beat of the measure. A sarabande is usually the third movement in a dance suite.

SARABANDE

Arcangelo Corelli (1653–1713)

- This sarabande contains two trills in measures 4 and 15. A **trill (tr.)** is an even alternation of two adjacent tones. Play the trills as written out in small notes.

MINUET IN G

Johann Sebastian Bach (1685–1750)

Allegretto

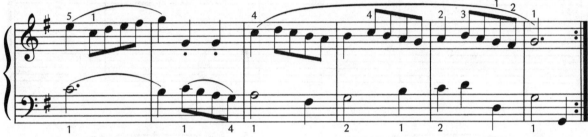

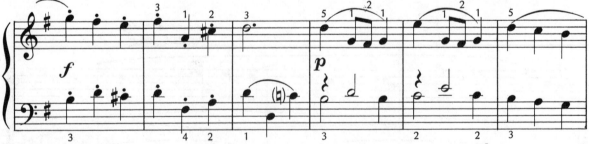

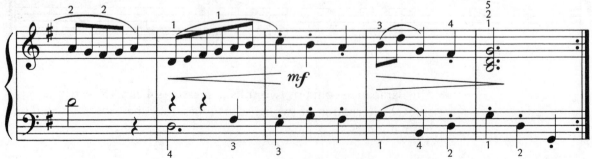

GERMAN DANCE

Franz Joseph Haydn (1732–1809)

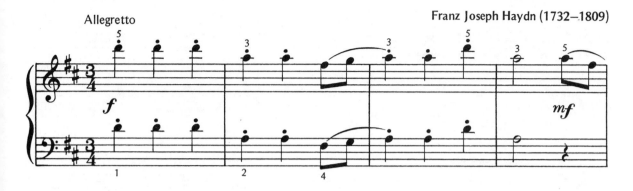

ALLEGRO

Wolfgang Amadeus Mozart

Allegro giocoso

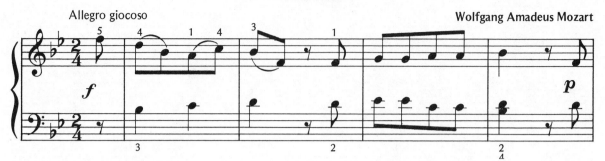

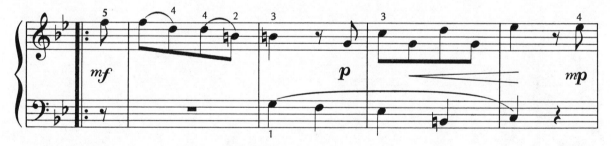

An **écossaise** is an English country dance of the eighteenth and early nineteenth century.

ÉCOSSAISE

Ludwig van Beethoven

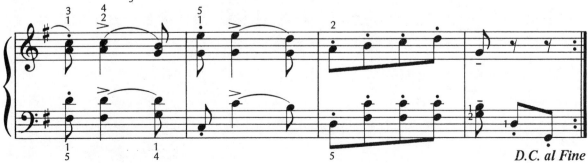

D.C. al Fine

THEME from Six Variations on "Nel cor più non mi sento"

Ludwig van Beethoven

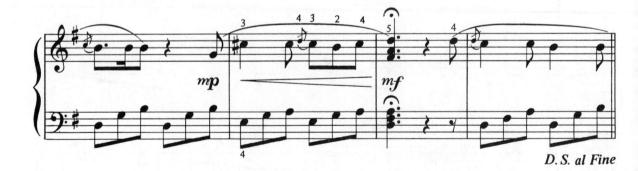

- **D.S.** is an abbreviation of **dal segno,** which means to repeat from the sign 𝄋.

The 24 Chopin Preludes are short character pieces, each of them establishing and maintaining a particular mood.

PRELUDE IN A, Op. 28, No. 7

Frédéric Chopin (1810–1849)

■ **Ped. simile** means to pedal in the same manner as previously marked.

HUMMING SONG (from 43 Piano Pieces for the Young, Op. 68)

Robert Schumann (1810–1851)

SOLDIER'S MARCH
(from Kinderscenen, Op. 15)

Robert Schumann

One day in Weimar the composer Franz Liszt saw Madame Pelet-Narbonne, a very plump and rather awkward lady, riding the carrousel at a visiting carnival. Liszt burst into the home of friends and reported that he had seen something extremely funny. He then sat down at the piano and improvised a musical sketch of the experience. His friends were so delighted that they urged Liszt to write it down, which he did. And that is the original of *Carrousel de Madame Pelet-Narbonne*.

CARROUSEL DE MADAME PELET-NARBONNE

Franz Liszt

ITALIAN SONG

Peter Ilich Tchaikovsky

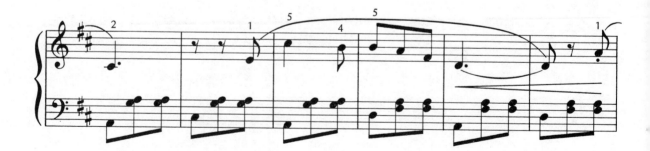

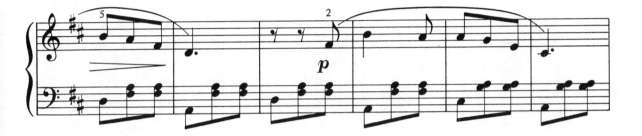

THE BEAR

Vladimir Rebikoff (1866–1920)

WALTZ (from Six Children's Pieces)

Dmitri Shostakovich (1906—1975)

CLOWNS

Dmitri Kabalevsky

CHILDREN'S GAME (from For Children, Vol. I)

Béla Bartók

Allegro moderato (♩ = 100)

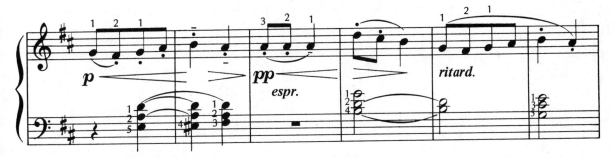

STREET GAMES

Elie Siegmeister (born 1909)

MOON DANCE
(No. 2 from *Mountain Idylls*)

Alan Hovhaness (born 1911)

Allegro (♩. = 100-120)

LULLABY

Very quiet (♩. = 46)

Norman dello Joio

A **capriccio** is a free-style composition, capricious and humorous in character.

CAPRICCIO

Vincent Persichetti

BULLDOZER

Forcefully

David Kraehenbuehl (born 1923)

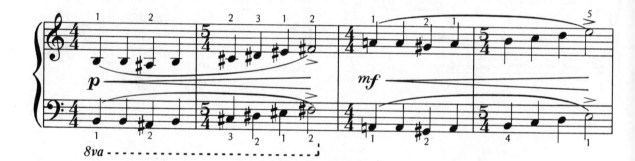

PERFORMANCE TERMS AND SYMBOLS

TEMPO TERMS
Presto   very rapidly
Vivace   quickly; spirited
Allegro   fast; lively
Allegretto   moderately fast; slower than Allegro
Moderato   moderately
Andantino   somewhat faster than Andante
Andante   at a walking pace
Adagio   rather slow; leisurely
Lento   slow
Largo   slow; broad
Grave   very slow; solemn

CHANGE-OF-TEMPO TERMS
A tempo   return to original tempo
Accelerando (*accel.*)   gradually increasing in tempo
Meno mosso   with less movement or motion
Più mosso   with more movement or motion
Rallentando (*rall.*)
Ritardando (*rit.*)   gradually slowing in tempo
Ritenuto (*riten.*)   immediately slowing in tempo; also used synonymously with rallentando and ritardando

DYNAMIC TERMS
Crescendo (*cresc.*)   gradually becoming louder
Decrescendo (*decresc.*)
Diminuendo (*dim., dimin.*)   gradually becoming softer
Pianissimo (*pp*)   very soft
Piano (*p*)   soft
Mezzo piano (*mp*)   moderately soft
Mezzo forte (*mf*)   moderately loud
Forte (*f*)   loud
Fortissimo (*ff*)   very loud

Sforzando (*sf., sfz.*)   strongly accented; with an emphatic stress

OTHER TERMS
Animato   animated; with spirit
Cantabile   in singing style
Coda   a concluding section of a few measures at the end of a composition
Con moto   with motion
Da capo (*D. C.*)   repeat from the beginning
Da capo al fine (*D. C. al fine*)   repeat from the beginning to *Fine*, the finish or end
Dal segno (*D. S.*)   repeat from the sign 𝄋
Dal segno al fine   repeat from the sign 𝄋 to *Fine*, the finish or end
Dolce   sweetly; delicately
Espressivo   expressively
Fine   the end of a composition
Giocoso   humorously; playfully
Grazioso   gracefully
Legato   smoothly; connected
Leggiero   lightly; nimbly
Maestoso   majestically; with dignity
Marcato   marked; stressed
Meno   less
Molto   much
Mosso   with agitated motion
Pesante   heavily
Più   more
Poco   little; a little
Scherzando   playfully
Sempre   always
Simile   in the same manner; similarly
Sostenuto   sustained
Troppo   much; too much

SYMBOLS AND SIGNS

> — ∧   accent mark—a sign placed under or over a note to indicate stress or emphasis

arpeggio—a sign placed before a chord to indicate that the notes are to be quickly rolled, one after the other, from bottom to top; harplike

c   a meter signature standing for common time; same as $\frac{4}{4}$

¢   a meter signature standing for cut time (alla breve); same as $\frac{2}{2}$

crescendo—gradually becoming louder

decrescendo or diminuendo—gradually becoming softer

1.   2.   first and second endings

fermata—indicates a hold or pause

glissando—a sweeping sound produced by pulling one or more fingernails rapidly over the keys

repeat signs

staccato mark—a dot placed under or over a note to indicate that the note is to be played detached, nonlegato

tremolo—a rapid alternation of two pitches of an interval larger than a second

LIST OF COMPOSITIONS

r.

INDEX